DON'T VOTE!

It Just Encourages the Bastards

DON'T VOTE!

It Just Encourages the Bastards

P. J. O'Rourke

Grove Press

First published in the United States of America in 2010 by
Grove/Atlantic Inc.

First published in Great Britain in 2010 by Grove Press,
an imprint of Grove/Atlantic Inc.

Every effoi   ight-holders.
The publis   ons or rectify
any mista   pportunity.

A CIP r   h Library.

Hardback ISBN 978 1 84887 942 3
Trade paperback ISBN 978 1 84887 906 5

Printed in Great Britain by the MPG Books Group

Grove Press
Ormond House
26-27 Boswell Street
London
WC1N 3JZ

www.groveatlantic.com

To my wife, Christina,
for her encouragement of this particular bastard
and for not imposing term limits

Contents

Acknowledgements

The title belongs to the great American political consultant, campaign strategist, advance man, and political prankster Dick Tuck. More than thirty years ago Dick told me that "Don't vote—it just encourages the bastards" was a favorite saying of his mother.

Dick Tuck was the Nemesis of Dick Nixon. At the first Nixon–Kennedy debate Tuck hired an old lady to get in front of the TV cameras wearing a Nixon button and throw her arms around the sweaty candidate who thought he'd bested his young opponent. "Don't worry, son," the old lady said loudly. "He beat you now, but you'll get him next time."

Tuck did some of his best work for the Kennedys, in particular the most estimable of them, Robert. Dick, I apologize for any harsh words about my fellow bogtrotters in the following pages. Although Tuck and I are, politically, an aisle apart, I've never had a partisan argument with him. Who could argue with the Nemesis of Dick Nixon?

Along with some jokes, this book is a work of political theory. As such it is not too original, and I mean that in a good way. Nothing is worse than a too original political theory except perhaps a too original cookbook. "Bring water to a boil and immerse live pythons."

To call an artist derivative is an insult.[1] To call a political theorist derivative is to admit that he or she has paid some attention to the eon of human political activity from which political theory derives.

Any reader who notices my use of the phrase "politics is an arrangement among persons" (or my use of the phrase "It's not a thinking man's game") may suspect that *Don't Vote* is a gloss or a glib exposition upon Michael Oakeshott's 1947 essay "Rationalism in Politics."[2] And that's true. Or I think maybe it's true. Twenty years of intermittent efforts were required for me to push my way through the prose brambles of Oakeshott's thesis. What you read here may be a passage of thought, or it may be a record of scratched mental tissue and torn ideological clothing resulting from an attempt to follow in Oakeshott's footsteps.

There are other writings that should be consulted for smarter versions of what I've written. *Novus Ordo Seclorum— The Intellectual Origins of the Constitution* by Forrest McDonald delivers what it promises it will. Adam Smith's *The Theory of Moral Sentiments* was the best work (and still is) of moral philosophy available as the moral philosophy of America was being formed. McDonald believes that *The Theory of Moral Sentiments* and *The Wealth of Nations* were the dominant flavorings to the broth of intellect in which America's founders stewed. (A silly metaphor but one of the pleasures an author takes in writing acknowledgements is knowing that they go to press lightly edited.)

---

1. I don't know why. Goethe's *Faust* is derivative. Gertrude Stein's *Tender Buttons* is awfully original.
2. Oakeshott's exact words: "Politics I take to be the activity of attending to the general arrangements of a set of people whom chance or choice have brought together." The definition is not, in fact, from "Rationalism in Politics" but from his Inaugural Lecture at the London School of Economics, delivered in 1950.

Thomas Paine is a political theorist whom I love for his sheer irksomeness to authority.[3] All there really is to say about the politics of liberty is contained in Paine's dictum "man has no property in man." But I have a crumbling, old collection of Paine's work (cover price 50¢) where, in a windy introduction by John Dos Passos, Paine's limitations are inadvertently pointed out. Dos Passos damns Paine by praising his "faith in man's unaided reason." A fellow hated by both the king of England and Robespierre and distrusted by John Adams—surely there was more to Paine than that.

Thomas Paine by Craig Nelson and *Thomas Paine's Rights of Man* by Christopher Hitchens gave me a better understanding of one Tom. And Hitchens's *Thomas Jefferson: Author of America* shed light on the complications of another. That book also ends with a splendid line of Christopher's, which I meant to find a place for in this book. Here will have to suffice: "History is a tragedy and not a morality tale."

While randomly pulling books from my reference shelf to look up some small historical matter I made the happy find of Hugh Brogan's *The Penguin History of the United States of America*. My copy was published in England in 1990, and I seem to have owned but not consulted it for a score of years. Brogan turns out to have a discerning eye for the manifold threads of populism in American politics. I thank him for an improved comprehension of Jacksonian Democrats, Radical Republicans, Greenbackers, and Progressives.

As to populism, I was holding forth in a lecture hall not long ago and, in answer to a question about the Tea Party movement,

---

3. I also like his spotty education. And here I'd like to thank Ramona Bass who, while reading a rough manuscript of my book, e-mailed me to point out that Paine's name is customarily spelled with an "e."

I said, "At least they aren't demanding any further positive rights from government. Name me another American populist group that hasn't demanded new positive rights." A voice from the crowd called out, "The Whiskey Rebellion!" Point taken.

For the concept of positive and negative rights, I—and all the rest of us—owe gratitude to Isaiah Berlin and his 1959 book *Two Concepts of Liberty*.

When I'm faced with political-economy conundrums (and political economy seems to contain nothing else), I fall back on a few works filled with common sense: *The Road to Serfdom* by Friedrich Hayek, *Economics in One Lesson* by Henry Hazlitt, *Capitalism and Freedom* by Milton Friedman, and *Free to Choose* by Milton and Rose Friedman.

These books are moral as well as material guides. Dr. Larry Arnn, president of Hillsdale College, once had an argument with Milton Friedman on this point. It went something like this:

> Arnn: "*Free to Choose* is a deeply moral book."
> Friedman: "*Free to Choose* is a book of practical economics."
> Arnn: "It's a moral book."
> Friedman: "It's a practical book."
> Arnn: "It's a moral book."
> Friedman: "I wrote it, and I say it's a book of practical economics."
> Arnn: "Once you write it, it isn't yours anymore. I read it, and I say it's a moral book."

When I become confused by economic theory (and is there any other way to be?), I turn to *New Ideas from Dead Economists* by Todd Buchholz. He quickly and cogently explains the ideas of dead economists and tells us why to hope that most of them stay dead.

Then there is a book that provides a negative lesson. Much as I admire the stylings of H. L. Mencken, it is his worst work, *Notes on Democracy*, that I find inspiring. *Notes* was published in 1926 and is an extended bitch on the subject. All Mencken can manage by way of complimenting democracy is to ask, "Is it inordinately wasteful, extravagant, dishonest? Then so is every other form of government: all alike are enemies to laborious and virtuous men." That's crap. Witness mankind's experiences with "every other form of government." Witness the alternatives to democracy on offer the very year *Notes* came out: Russia's communism, Italy's fascism, the whiff of mob rule in Britain's general strike.

One more writer upon whom I've relied heavily—though he's neither profound nor consistent—is me. Writing about politics after an adulthood spent writing about politics would be impossible without a certain amount of self-plagiarism.

Some phrases, sentences, and the occasional paragraph from my previous books reappear in this one. In *Parliament of Whores, All the Trouble in the World, Eat the Rich,* and *On The Wealth of Nations* I tried, in different contexts, to think through some of the same problems I've tried to think through here. Sometimes you say things as well as you can and when it's time to say the same thing the person you end up quoting is you.

"He must be a poor creature who does not often repeat himself," said Oliver Wendell Holmes. "Imagine the author of the excellent piece of advice, 'Know thyself,' never alluding to that sentiment again." And I've used that before too, in *The CEO of the Sofa*. Only once, however, do I lift a long passage from a volume of my own. In 1993 I wrote an op-ed for *The Wall Street Journal* saying what I thought of Hillary Clinton's health care reform proposal. I included this in a 1995 collection, *Age and Guile*. As a testimony to the circles—per Dante's *Inferno*—that politics runs around in, I changed one name and a couple of numbers and this was what I thought of Barack Obama's health care reform proposal.

Besides cribs from my books, at least twenty-seven essays and speeches written over the past fifteen years have served as rough drafts for parts of *Don't Vote*.

I am very grateful to *The Weekly Standard* where I've had a happy home since it was founded in 1995. I thank everyone on its staff from William Kristol and Fred Barnes at the top of the masthead to the most temporary of interns who politely pretend to know who I am when I phone the office. It is a pleasure working with all of you. And for adding ideas to my head and subtracting solecisms from my prose I give specific thanks to deputy editor Richard Starr, literary editor Philip Terzian, managing editor Claudia Anderson, and my oldest friend in Washington, senior editor Andrew Ferguson.

I also had ample opportunities to talk, think, and write about politics at *The Atlantic* under the editorship of Cullen Murphy and before that under the editorship of the late and much-missed Michael Kelly.

The chapter "Why I'm Right" appeared in the book *Why I Turned Right,* edited by the brilliant Mary Eberstadt, mother of my goddaughter, Alexandra.

"The End of the American Automobile Industry" chapter I owe to an assignment from *The Wall Street Journal.*

Jim Denton, my other oldest friend in Washington and the publisher of *World Affairs,* encouraged me to plunge into the morass of foreign policy.

Additional articles from which I've drawn material appeared in *Forbes,* the *Financial Times,* and, of all places, *Rolling Stone* where for some reason Bill Greider and I were allowed to conduct a months-long left vs. right debate in print, doubtless to the utter mystification of the *Rolling Stone* target demographic. (Bill's a great guy—wrong about everything, but a great guy.)

For almost thirty years I've been working with—well, he's done all the working—Don Epstein at the Greater Talent Network lecture agency. Through the kind and diligent efforts of Don and everyone at GTN I've had the opportunity to try out various political ideas and opinions on lecture audiences around the county. (No audience members were harmed in these experiments. As far as I know.)

When the idea for this book was larval, Larry Arnn listened attentively to my description of the grub.

Greg Lindsay, executive director of The Center for Independent Study, invited me and my family to Australia and New Zealand in 2009. There Greg and his family showed us splendid hospitality. (Greg, Tina is still Googling "How to remove red wine stains from white lamb's wool rugs.") The talks that I gave in Sydney, Canberra, Perth, and Wellington would, through no fault of Greg's, evolve into the opening chapters of *Don't Vote*.

Thanks also to John Green and his family for making our antipodean journey so excellent (for everything except white lamb's wool rugs).

The Cato Institute, that most thoughtful of Washington think tanks, has been providing me with research support—not to mention the moral kind—since the 1980s. There is no one working at Cato who hasn't, in some way, helped form my political ideas. To name a very few of them:

executive vice president David Boaz, especially for his book *Libertarianism: A Primer* and for his editorship of *The Libertarian Reader*.

xvi   ACKNOWLEDGEMENTS

Tom Palmer and Roger Pilon for their knowledge and understanding of constitutionalism.

Peter Van Doren, editor of Cato's invaluable antiregulatory *Regulation* magazine.

Jerry Taylor, who knows everything about resources and the squandering of them, which government is so good at.

Michael Tanner, Michael F. Cannon, and Aaron Yelowitz, without whose mastery of facts and figures I could not have written the health care chapter.

And, of course, Ed Crane, Cato's president-for-life, who has bestowed upon me the title "Mencken Research Fellow" at Cato. I'm honored even though I'm pretty sure Ed has read Mencken's *Notes on Democracy*.

Max Pappas was my assistant a decade ago and has done well anyway. He now occupies the post of vice president, public policy, at FreedomWorks. Max researched the origins of modern terrorism, and I apologize for taking ten years to put his research to use. It was also Max who walked me through the blind alleys of ratiocination behind campaign-finance reform and who explained to me what the hell the recent Supreme Court ruling on the subject was all about.

Richard Pipes, the preeminent historian of Russia and the Russian revolution, is a good friend and also a great teacher about the process by which reform turns to radicalism and radicalism turns to riot. I am deeply in debt to his book *Property and Freedom*, the most powerful argument for linking these social goods since Adam Smith's.

It was Charlie Glass who, more than a quarter-century ago, showed me through the ruins of Lebanon and let me see that, when we call the American political system "highly polarized," "chaotic," and "corrupt," we are full of shit. Charlie and I don't usually agree about politics, but it is my hope that he'll be able to get through at least a few chapters of this book before he writes to tell me that I remain a right-wing nut.

Jay Winik confirmed my hunch that Alexander Hamilton never recanted his objections to the first ten amendments to the U.S. Constitution. "But," wrote Jay, "I also strongly suspect that, like most of the other founders, he made peace with the Bill of Rights."

Nick Eberstadt provided me with, among many other things, an educated guess at the body count from Mao's "let a hundred flowers bloom" pogrom.

Kudos to Neil Hudley for rediscovering Milton Friedman's radio interviews from the Paleolithic (1970's) era of media.

Tim Baney pointed out the number of gun murders (none) in North Dakota, a state with notoriously lax gun-control laws.

Ed Mallon and Des Desvernine are doing important ongoing undercover work, therefore I cannot name them publically.

Candles for Men—"Mandles"—was the idea of Alex Vogel. The complete range of scents available as soon as Alex gets his start-up capital: Beer, Cigars, Old Dog, Spilled Bourbon, Gear Oil, Pool Hall, Frying Meat, Grass Clippings, Charcoal Smoke, Chainsaw Exhaust, Canvas Tarpaulin, and Trout.

Michael Gewirz had the savvy notion for marketing Home Colonoscopy Kits.

"Motorized cupholders" is a quip I stole from Lee Bass. Lee will know what I mean when I say, "After finishing this book I need to sit down for a moment and sort things out."

I swiped the line about Japan sticking its economy "where the rising sun never shines" from my old friend Dave Garcia in Hong Kong.

James A. Weiner, Foreign Service Officer (Ret.), provided me with a joke that will go unspecified.

My assistant, Phoebe Bunker, spent many long hours digging up obscure and abstruse research material for this book. She also spent many more and much longer hours inputting and outputting and (for all I know) shot putting the manuscript because I don't even know which end of a computer to stick the eight-track cassette into. Phoebe, you were very good-natured about it all.

The dust cover photo was shot with style and flair by James Kegley, who is not to be blamed for his subject's looks (or attire —that being the author's idea on the theory that the only real benefit of being over sixty is a perfect freedom to injure one's own dignity, to the extent that time hasn't done the job already).

The author would look even more frightful if it hadn't been for the ministrations of stylist Janis Heffron and of photographer's assistant Mike Stargill who kept moving the lights around in an attempt to keep the cover photo from looking like a portrait of Uncle Samosaurus.

At the behest of my excellent friend Frank Saul, Washington's Hay-Adams Hotel lent us a room for the photo shoot. Jenny Niessen made us comfortable there, for which we thank her. You should stay at the Hay-Adams even if you live in Washington already. It's so close to the White House that you can see the president sneak a smoke, but not so close that he can lecture you on health care reform and financial regulation.

Grove/Atlantic has remained a patient and understanding publisher. Chief executive Morgan Entrekin, with whom my friendship dates back to the 1970s, has published all but one of my books and he reissued that one. Thank you Morgan, and thank you Eric Price for keeping Grove/Atlantic functioning,

Charles Rue Woods for keeping it looking good, Deb Seager and Scott Manning for keeping it publicized, Don Kennison for un-mangling my spelling and grammar, managing editor Michael Hornburg for managing, Sue Cole for making sure somebody remembered to send the book to the printer, and to Andrew Robinton and every other Grove/Atlantic literary light.

And lastly I want to thank my wife, Tina, for fifteen years of happiness, which is none of the reader's business. More to the point I want to thank her for the editorial targeting she did on *Don't Vote*. Tina undertook a careful re-aiming of my 12 gauge, open bore, scatter-shot approach to my subject. She convinced me to use full choke in both barrels on politics. I've got a bead on the thing now, Honey. And I promise I won't ask you to clean or cook it.

Apologia Pro !%@& Sua

I beg forgiveness from the reader for the vulgar language in this book. Politics is a vulgar fucking subject. I have resorted to barnyard words because of the amount of bullshit, horseshit, and chickenshit involved in politics. I'm sorry I can't devise a more polite mode of expression. I can only blame myself. It is possible, I suppose, to take a decorous approach to politics. But I'm reminded of the American guest at a dinner in one of the great houses of Britain. The American was seated to the left of a very grand and fat old duchess and an Englishman was seated on her right. During the soup course the duchess farted. The Englishman, taking chivalrous responsibility, said, "I beg your pardon." During the fish course the duchess farted again, louder than before. Once more, the Englishman said, "I beg your pardon." Then, during the meat course, the duchess cut loose with a tremendous, resounding blast. The Englishman said, "I beg—"

"No, no," the American interrupted. "This one's on me."

PART I

The Sex, Death, and Boredom Theory of Politics

The man of system . . . is apt to be very wise in his own conceit; and is often so enamored with the supposed beauty of his own ideal plan of government, that he cannot suffer the smallest deviation from any part of it.

—Adam Smith

"Scientific socialism" would hold especial attraction for intellectuals by promising to replace spontaneous and messy life with a rational order of which they would be the interpreters and mentors.

—Richard Pipes

Here's a good rule of thumb:
Too clever is dumb.

—Ogden Nash

1

Kill Fuck Marry

Having been a political commentator of one kind or another since 1970, it has occurred to me to ask: What the hell have I been talking about for forty years?

It's a surprisingly difficult question to answer. One subject has been power, the skull beneath the skin of politics. Sometimes we get flayed completely and there's nothing left but a pile of skulls. Then there's freedom. From my addlepated hippie youth to my right-wing grouch maturity, I've been a fan of freedom, particularly my own. Furthermore, because I've always lived in a nation that is self-ruled (if often by selfish selves) and that is under the rule of law (if often legally unruly), responsibility, too, has been a topic, although I dislike taking any.

Power, freedom, and responsibility are the trinity of politics in a free and democratic country. But it's hard to know how to go about understanding this triad. We are so passionate about our politics. And how do passionate affairs end? In a passion, usually. In a crime of passion, sometimes. Occasionally they turn into stable, permanent, connubial relationships, which is to say endless, peevish quarrels.

How should the political institutions of America be approached? Do we overthrow them with violence? Do we screw around with them while they screw around with us? Or do we try to build something that's lasting and boring, worthy and annoying, marvelously virtuous and at the same time dreadfully stifling?

No wonder most of my fellow political commentators and I have preferred to rave about politics rather than consider them. It's human nature—at least among free and democratic humans—to be angry, confused, and instinctual about politics. So how do we go about creating a set of political principles that don't suck? We need a reasonable, reasonably precise, and reasonably well reasoned way to look at political institutions, political policies, and politicians. There is ample evidence of what happens when such principles are lacking: Somalia.

Power, freedom, and responsibility are not principles in and of themselves; they're perspectives. But we can use these three ways of looking at things to analyze politics. The game "Kill Fuck Marry" comes to us, as far as anyone can tell, from late-night giggle sessions at all-girls boarding schools. Take three political institutions that seem to occupy different vertices in the triangulation of power, freedom, and responsibility. Or, because it's more fun, take three politicians. For instance, the Kennedy brothers: charismatic Jack, conscientious Bobby, and Teddy with a lampshade on his head. Obviously, we kill Ted, fuck Jack, and marry Bobby.

If choosing among martyred (plus cancer-stricken) Kennedys seems tasteless, we can use the 1992 U.S. presidential candidates, who, for example's sake, were exemplary. We kill Ross Perot. We could hardly avoid a fuck from Bill Clinton. And we marry kindly, old George H. W. Bush.

The game's outcome is not always certain (per our mysterious elopement with Bill instead of our church wedding with

George). In the case of the 2000 presidential election people of goodwill were evenly divided about whether to fuck Al Gore or marry George W., although I believe we all agreed on killing Ralph Nader.

I won't venture any answers involving more recent elections for fear of attracting attention (hard as that sometimes seems) from the Secret Service. But the game works on the parts of government as well as it does on the politicians who run them. We kill the postal service, fuck the Department of Health and Human Services, and marry the armed forces. The same goes with government policies: fuck agricultural subsidies, marry Social Security, and health care reform kills us.

Try "Kill Fuck Marry" at your next cocktail party if you want the people you invited never to speak to one another again.

2

Politics Makes Us Free

And We're Worth It

When I first began to think about politics—when mastodons and Nixon roamed the earth—I was obsessed with freedom. I had a messy idea of freedom at the time, but I had the tidy idea that freedom was the central issue of politics.

I loved politics. Many young people do—kids can spot a means of gain without merit. (This may be the reason professional politicians retain a certain youthful zest; Strom Thurmond was the boyo right down to his last senile moment.) I was wrong about the lovable nature of politics, and even at twenty-three I probably suspected I was wrong. But I was sure I was right about the preeminent place of freedom in a political system.

Freedom is a personal ideal. Because politics is an arrangement among persons, we can plausibly assume that freedom is a political ideal. Our favorite political idealists think so. They've been unanimous on the subject since Jean-Jacques Rousseau convinced polite society that human bondage was in bad taste and John Locke showed the divine right of kings to be a royal pain.

The signers of the Declaration of Independence declared us to be residents of "Free and Independent States." John Adams demanded, "Let me have a country, and that a free country." Tom Paine warned that "Freedom hath been hunted round the globe." And he exhorted us to "receive the fugitive and prepare in time an asylum for mankind." Calling America an asylum may have been a poor choice of words, or not. Thomas Jefferson, in his first inaugural address, preached "Freedom of religion; freedom of the press, and freedom of person." Jefferson was quite free with the person of Sally Hemings. And a dinner toast from Revolutionary War general John Stark bestowed upon New Hampshire a license plate motto that must puzzle advocates of highway safety: "Live Free or Die."

With *Bartlett's Familiar Quotations* as a useful gauge of what we think we think, we find that Emerson poetized, "For what avail the plow or sail, or land or life, if freedom fail?" Hegel weighed in, "The history of the world is none other than the progress of the consciousness of freedom." As unlikely a character as the crackpot Nietzsche had something to say: "Liberal institutions straightway cease from being liberal the moment they are soundly established: once this is attained no more grievous and more thorough enemies of freedom exist than liberal institutions." The UN Commission on Human Rights comes to mind.

We can survey the arts, where mankind is most blatant in its truths, and find artists taking the broadest liberties. (They are especially free with the use of fate as a plot device.) We can peruse philosophy, where mankind is less truthful, and not hear freedom denied by anything except free thinking. Theology makes sporadic arguments against free will, with which the devout are freely willing to concur. Science is deterministic and its special needs stepsister social science is more so. But people are free to pick and choose among the determinations of science until they find something they like. I give you Al Gore and you can have him. Perhaps there are scientists who make a sound case for the inevitabilities of biology and such. But we don't know what these geniuses are talking about and very likely neither do they. For example, the important biologist Richard Dawkins has written a book, *The God Delusion,* in which he uses predestinarian atheism to argue that Richard Dawkins is the closest thing to a superior being in the known universe.

The theoretical (as opposed to practical) enemies of freedom are feeble opponents. And we are all but overrun by theoretical allies in freedom's cause. We've got collaborators in the fight for freedom that we don't even want. "The proletarians have nothing to lose but their chains" is the penultimate sentence of the *Communist Manifesto.* And a creepy echo of it can be heard in the refrain of Kris Kristofferson's "Me and Bobby McGee." Mao announced, "Letting a hundred flowers blossom and a hundred schools of thought contend is the policy..." Half a million people died in those ellipses.

If we were to give out the proverbial "a word to the wise," the sagacity-testing utterance with which to provide the sages would be "freedom." In the unabridged *Oxford English Dictionary* the noun has fifteen definitions and the adjective "free" has thirty-six. These definitions, along with their usage citations, occupy 189¼ column inches of small and smaller type.

Peter Roget (1779–1869), of *Roget's Thesaurus,* was a physician, a scientist, the secretary of the Royal Society for more than twenty years, and an exhaustingly systematic thinker. He designed his thesaurus (Greek for "treasury") as a reverse dictionary. Instead of listing words and giving their meanings, he listed meanings and gave words for them. Under the heading "freedom" there are more than four hundred entries in twenty-one categories. And "freedom" is only one of the twenty-three headings in *Roget's* "Section I, General Intersocial Volition" of "Division II, Intersocial Volition" of "Class Five, Volition." It's hard to know whether or not to be thankful that Peter Roget's obsessive-compulsive disorder meds hadn't been invented.

Among the various types and kinds of general intersocial volition, about ten have something to do with political freedom.

freedom in the abstract
autonomy
enfranchisement
toleration
frankness
leisure
laxity
abandon
opportunity
privilege

Several of these may seem beside the point. But "frank," for instance, is from the Old French *franc,* meaning free. We can be frank with the president of the United States. We can honestly and openly say what we think to him. And what we think of him. But in all our name-calling the name we call our president that sticks is "Mr." He's not "Your Excellency" or "Your Highness," nor do we kowtow, genuflect, or curtsy to him. Callisthenes, the great-nephew of Aristotle, plotted to kill Alexander the Great rather than prostrate himself in the Persian manner to the conqueror of the known world. It's probably just as well that our current president forgoes even a handshake with Fox News.

Then there are the freedoms of leisure, laxity, and wild abandon. Anyone who thinks these have nothing to do with democracy hasn't met the demos. Also, it was not so long ago, during the great political demonstrations of the 1960s, that I was risking my neck—well, risking a conk on the head and a snootful of tear gas—in the battle to create a utopian society where I could lie around all day, utterly heedless and high as a kite.

Freedom, of course, may be considered as an abstraction. I was young enough to be highly abstracted—not to say stoned— when I began to think about freedom. But I wasn't old enough to think. Therefore I can tell you nothing about my abstract thinking on the subject. And so can't a lot of other people, because there are languages in which the word "freedom" doesn't exist. (Not surprising if you think about some of the places languages are spoken.) Richard Pipes, emeritus professor of Russian history at Harvard, who is fluent in a number of tongues himself, makes this point in his book *Property and Freedom* (a perspicacious analysis of what the title says).

Professor Pipes cites the work of M. I. Finley, preeminent historian of classical antiquity (and, incidentally, a Marxist, something Richard Pipes is the opposite of). Finley wrote, "It is impossible to translate the word 'freedom,' *eleutheris* in Greek, *libertas* in Latin, or 'free man,' into any ancient Near Eastern language, including Hebrew, or into any Far Eastern language either, for that matter." Indeed, when the Japanese first encountered Western notions they were hard put to translate "freedom" and ended up using the word *jiyu,* which means something like "getting jiggy with it."

Freedom and liberty themselves don't have quite the same meaning. "Free" is derived from the Indo-European root *pri,* to love. The *p* becomes *f* in Germanic languages, thus *fri* in Old German and *freo* in Old English. The original sense of the adjective was "dear," and it was used to describe those members of a household who had a kinship relation to the master of the house. Since at least the reign of King Alfred the Great, ruled 871–899, the primary definition of "free" has been "not in bondage." You're free because . . . Who loves ya, Baby?

Liberty is probably the better word;[1] its source is in the Indo-European *leudh*, "to mount up, grow." Hence Latin for children, *liberi,* and German for populace, *Leute.* We the people make *leudh* into *eleutheris* and *libertas.*

Yet, the first definition of "liberty" in English is, once again, "exemption or release from bondage." Whatever we mean by our abstract statements about freedom and liberty, the most meaningful thing we're stating is that mankind has a sickening history of slavery.

Enfranchisement is the lively, fortunate, and honorable freedom, for the sake of which our political ancestors pledged their lives, their fortunes, and their sacred honor. Nothing concerning the goal of enfranchisement is ignoble except its attainment. Among those who choose the congressmen, senators, and

---

1. But "freedom" is less highfalutin and more of an Americanism. Theodore Parker, a prominent abolitionist, may be partly responsible for the American usage. He is certainly responsible for the American definition of democracy. Parker gave a series of speeches in Boston in the 1850s. Abraham Lincoln's law partner William Herndon attended one of these talks and gave the following transcript to Lincoln, to obvious effect.

A democracy—that is a government of all the people, by all the people, for all the people; of course, a government of the principles of eternal justice, the unchanging law of God; for shortness' sake I will call it the idea of Freedom.

presidents of the United States we now include people who are not considered mature and responsible enough to have a beer. (If it's any comfort, we should remind ourselves of the purpose of voting. We don't vote to elect great persons to office. They're not that great. We vote to throw the bastards out.)

Toleration is the best comfort of a free life for most people most of the time, especially if they experience as well as practice it. But tolerance is of minor interest to politics. Politics aspires to a big, positive role in things. And the role of politics in toleration is small except in the usually negative actions of keeping the peace. Yet it was two consummate American politicians who supplied us with a model for the universal formulation of tolerance: "Mind your own business and keep your hands to yourself." These may be rightly called the Bill and Hillary Clinton Rules. Hillary, mind your own business. Bill, keep your hands to yourself.

The ontological freedom known as autonomy isn't part of practical politics, it's all of practical politics—imposing my will and thwarting yours. If the actions of mankind and the events of history turn out to have been foreordained it will be a good joke on politics.

This leaves us with the nub or butt end of politicking: privilege and opportunity. Ignore everything politicians say about opportunity. They're lying. When politicians tout "opportunity" either they are trying to help voters disguise an extortion as a gift or they are the groom of government complimenting the bride of private property while in bed with the socialist maid of honor. And ignore all of politicians' sniffing at and scorn for privilege. Privilege and opportunity are the names for rights—opportunity being rights you'd like to get and privilege being rights you'd like someone else to surrender. A politician doesn't ask if he may have the privilege of a dance; he says he has a right to it.

★   ★   ★

Our gassing about our rights is almost equal to our gassing about our freedoms when we're bent over and puffed full of air concerning our form of government. We're inordinately proud of the Bill of Rights. But it's an odd document.

The First and Sixth Amendments are straightforward enough, reassuring us that we may pray (OMG!), Twitter, kvetch, and be tried in the same court as O. J. Simpson. And the Fifth Amendment says that when we screw up big time we don't have to give our version—like anybody's going to believe us. But the Second Amendment is woefully confusing. (Not that it confuses *me* about gun ownership, in case you were considering a mugging to get my Jitterbug mobile phone.) The principal right that the Second Amendment seems to guarantee is the right to be a soldier. To judge by our various episodes of national conscription—Civil War, World War I, World War II, Korea, Vietnam—this is a right we sometimes have to force people to enjoy.

According to the Third Amendment the Pentagon can't just randomly send the U.S. Marines to sleep on our fold-out couch. This is something that, as a home owner, you'd think would be obvious. Although, in fairness, there are people elsewhere who wish they had an amendment keeping the Marines out of their house.

The Third Amendment and the Seventh Amendment (concerning jury appeals), are undercut by weasel words: "but in a manner to be prescribed by law" and "otherwise . . . than according to the rules of the common law." The Fourth Amendment (mandating warrants) and the Eighth Amendment (limiting punishments) include strange pairs of modifiers—"unreasonable" and "probable," "cruel" and "unusual"—better suited to a drunken description of my first marriage than to a sober writ of law.

And the message of the Ninth and Tenth Amendments is: You have other rights but you have to guess what they are.

There was opposition to the Bill of Rights. The modern mind expects it to have come from slave owners. But this is too modern. Support for the first ten amendments had little to do with dictionary definitions of freedom and liberty and a great deal to do with qualms that old-line Revolutionary patriots—including Sam Adams—had about the new federal government. Alexander Hamilton, who had other qualms, made a case against the Bill of Rights in that supposed ur-text of American freedoms *The Federalist Papers,* in number 84.

Hamilton put forth various arguments opposing the addition of any bill of rights to the U.S. Constitution. Some of the arguments were weak. Hamilton claimed that the Constitution, as it was, affirmed and maintained the ancient protections of individual liberty embodied in British common law. Maybe. But a less dangerous and expensive way to retain British common law had been available in 1776. Hamilton claimed that previous, precedent-setting bills of rights, starting with the Magna Carta, were merely bargains between a sovereign and his subjects about a ruler's prerogatives. Hamilton felt that no such sharp dealing and unseemly horse trading was necessary in a social contract freely made among equals. But if Nietzsche was right about what liberal institutions do once they're institutionalized—and there's no evidence he wasn't—then Hamilton was wrong. And Hamilton believed the Constitution already included the most important safeguards of freedom: establishment of habeas corpus, prohibition of ex post facto laws, and a ban on titles of nobility. Hamilton was listing the principal instruments in the tyranny tool chest of his era. He didn't foresee the future inventions of oppression such as ethnic cleansing, even though ethnic cleansing of North America was well under way at the time the *Federalist* essays were written.

But Hamilton's other objections to the Bill of Rights were prescient. Don't give the government ideas, he warned.

> Why, for instance, should it be said that the liberty of the press shall not be restrained, when no power is given by which restrictions may be imposed? I will not contend that such a provision would confer a regulating power; but it is evident that it would furnish, to men disposed to usurp, a plausible pretense for claiming that power. They might urge . . . the provision against restraining the liberty of the press afforded a clear implication that a power to prescribe proper regulations concerning it was intended to be vested in the national government.

And now we have not only the FCC's naughty involvement in Janet Jackson's wardrobe malfunction but also the gross obscenities of binding and gagging displayed in America's campaign finance legislation.[2]

Hamilton said that, in the matter of defining a right, "Who can give it any definition which would not leave the utmost

---

2. Although, as I write, the Supreme Court has overruled some of this legislation. Corporations, as legal persons, turn out to have the same rights to free speech as we personal persons. Corporations are people? Who knew? This may explain how I got screwed by British Petroleum the other night after a few too many drinks at the Capital Grille.

latitude for evasion?" Not even God, if you note the various evasions practiced by believers since Genesis. Hamilton said the true security of our freedom "must altogether depend on public opinion, and on the general spirit of the people and of the government." Each of these can be rotten, and occasionally all of them are. Such an occasion arose just seven years after the Bill of Rights was ratified. The Sedition Act made it a federal crime to publish anything about Congress or the president that would bring them into "contempt or disrepute." In other words, the Sedition Act made it a federal crime to publish anything about Congress or the president.

Fortunately the Bill of Rights is flawed in its treatment of only one type of rights—opportunities. It doesn't meddle with the other type—privileges. Perhaps these two categories of rights should be known as "get-outa-here" rights and "gimme" rights or, as they're more usually called in political theory, negative rights and positive rights. The Bill of Rights (and "the idea of Freedom") is concerned mostly with our liberty to say, "I've got God, guns, and a big damn mouth, and if the jury finds me guilty, the judge will pay my bail!" This is a negative right—our right to be left alone, our freedom from interference, usually from government, but also from our fellow citizens when they want us to sober up, quit yelling, put the shotgun down, and go back into the house.

Politicians, in their hearts, are always tepid supporters of get-outa-here rights. For one thing, any and all legislators are being invited to leave. For another thing, strict adherence to negative rights would leave little scope for legislating, something legislators dearly love to do. Gimme rights are more politically alluring. This is how we find ourselves tempted with positive rights to education, housing, health care, a living wage, flood relief, high-speed Internet access, and all the kingdoms of the world, and all the glory of them.

Politicians show no signs of even knowing the difference between negative and positive rights. Blinded by the dazzle of anything that makes them popular, they honestly may not be able to tell. But there's evidence that a confusion of negative and positive rights originally was presented to the public with malice aforethought. President Franklin Roosevelt's "Four Freedoms" appear to be, at first glance, as natural, well matched, and tidy of composition as the Norman Rockwell illustrations for them.

1. Freedom of speech and expression
2. Freedom of religion
3. Freedom from want
4. Freedom from fear

But notice how the beggar, number 3, has been slipped in among the more respectable members of the Freedom family. "Want *what*?" we ask ourselves.

Saying, as Roosevelt did in his January 6, 1941, State of the Union address, that "We look forward to a world founded upon four essential human freedoms" and that one of these freedoms is "freedom from want" was not an expression of generosity. Declarations of positive rights never are. There were six million Jews in Europe who wanted nothing but a safe place to go.

Politicians are careless about promising positive rights and cynical about delivering them. Positive rights themselves, in turn, are absurdly expandable. The government gives me a right to get married. This shows I have a right to a good marriage, otherwise why bother giving it to me? My marriage is made a lot better by my children's right to day care, so the brats aren't in my face all day being deprived of their right to a nurturing developmental environment. Every child has the right to a happy childhood, so I have the right to happy children. Richer children are happier. Give me some of Angelina Jolie's.

The expense of all this makes politicians glad. They get to do the spending. Even negative rights aren't free. They entail a military, a constabulary, a judiciary, and a considerable expenditure of patience by our neighbors. But positive rights require no end of money, and money is the least of their cost. Every positive right means the transfer of goods and services from one group of citizens to another. The first group of citizens loses those goods and services, but all citizens lose the power that must be given to a political authority to enforce the transfer. Perhaps such transfers could be made voluntary. U.S. federal personal income tax receipts in 2008: $1,426,000,000,000. U.S. charitable contributions in 2008: $307,700,000. Perhaps not.

When rights consist of special privileges and material benefits, rights kill freedom. Wrong rights are the source of political power. It's not freedom but power that is the central issue in politics. Only an idiot wouldn't have seen that. And I was one.

At least I wasn't alone. In the latter two-thirds of the twentieth century, most of us who involved ourselves in democratic politics claimed that freedom was what we were up to. We claimed it for more than fifty years, from the time of our defeat in the Spanish civil war until the embarrassing moment when those authoritarians Ronald Reagan and Margaret Thatcher led us to victory in the cold war. Liberals, moderates, and even some conservatives considered the sweeping positive rights created by a half century of social welfare programs to be extensions of freedom, in the opportunity sense. People were being given the opportunity to, you know, not starve to death and stuff.

This wasn't an evil way of looking at things. And not all the programs were bad. But the electorate, the candidates, and we busybody pundits failed to properly scrutinize social welfare programs. It's not that we failed to examine whether the programs were needed or superfluous or well or poorly run. What we failed to look at was the enormous power being taken from persons and given to politics. We insisted on seeing politics through the lens of freedom, as if social legislation were a Polaroid print of quickly developing liberties. We listened only to the freedom track on the electoral stereo. We predicted the future of politics with a horoscope containing just the astrological sign Libra.

We weren't exactly wrong. Living in the midst of the civil rights struggle, during a cold war with one totalitarian ideology after a real war with another, we understood the value of freedom and the ugly alternative to democracy. But we didn't—or didn't want to—understand power. This was particularly true of my age cohort, the baby boom, and particularly evident in the way we reacted when politicians attempted to use their power to limit our freedom by conscripting us into a war in Vietnam. We challenged the establishment by growing our hair long and dressing like Bozo.

We're a pathetic bunch. And it didn't start with the Beatles, marijuana, and the pill. Recall the coonskin cap. I wore mine to school. Children of previous eras may have worn coonskin caps but they had to eat the raccoons first.

* ★ *

The baby boom's reluctance to attend to the issues of power resulted from the fact that we had some. Freedom *is* power, after all. And, as for freedom, we were full of it. We were the first middle-class-majority generation in history. We had the varieties of freedom that affluence provides, plus we had the other varieties of freedom provided by relaxation of religious convictions, sexual morality, etiquette, and good taste. The social institutions that enforce prudence and restraint had been through a world war, prohibition, depression, a world war part II, and Elvis. They were tired. We were allowed to fall under the power of our own freedoms. And we powered through them. Sixty years on we're still at it, letting not age, satiety, tedium, or erectile dysfunction stand in our way. Yet always at our back we hear the nagging thought that power comes with responsibility.

We don't want that. Has there ever been a generation—a nation, a civilization—more determined to evade responsibility? Probably. The ancient Romans sliced open animals and rummaged in their kidneys and livers in an attempt to avoid owning up to the consequences of empire and toga parties. The Greeks were forever running off to hear the irresponsible babble of the oracle at Delphi, the Larry King of her age. Maybe the Egyptians had an Oprah barge on the Nile where deceased pharaohs could fall to pieces and promise to become better mummies.

Nonetheless we and our contemporaries in the developed countries of the Western world have an impressive record of blame shifting, duty shirking, unaccountability, and refusal to admit guilt or, better, to readily confess to every kind of guilt then announce we've "moved on."

A gigantic global "Not My Fault" project has been undertaken with heroic amounts of time, effort, and money devoted to psychology, psychotherapy, sociology, sociopaths, social work, social sciences, Scientology, science, chemistry, the brain, brain chemistry, serotonin reuptake inhibitors, inhibitions, sex, sex therapy, talk therapy, talk radio, talk radio personalities, personality disorders, drugs, drug-free school zones, Internet addiction, economics, the Fed, PMS, SATs, IQ, DNA, evolution, abortion, divorce, no-fault car insurance, the Democratic Party, diagnosis of attention deficit disorder in small boys . . . The list goes on.

Neither freedom nor power is what I should have been obsessed with for all these years. But it's too late now. I'm a child of my era. And speaking of that era, here are three slogans from 1960s posters that never existed:

BLACK RESPONSIBILITY

SISTERHOOD IS RESPONSIBLE

RESPONSIBILITY TO THE PEOPLE

3

A Digression on Happiness

American exceptionalism annoys the world. Happiness is the source of the annoyance. Other countries are built upon battle, blood, nationality, culture, language, and territory. America is the exception. Our foundation is pursuit of happiness. It appears in the first sentence of the main body of America's IPO, the Declaration of Independence. Happiness is the one novel feature of the document. And this imaginative mission statement, that we're determined to pursue happiness, comes as something of a surprise after the noble boilerplate of our calls for life and liberty.

We can explore mankind's other covenants, treaties, conventions, protocols, compacts, and concordants, plus all the *corpus juris* of the world, written and unwritten, ancient and modern, and not find happiness.

No talk of happiness appears in England's Magna Carta. The French revolution's Declaration of the Rights of Man fails to address the subject. The European Union's proposed constitution never mentions happiness, although, at 485 pages, it mentions practically everything else including regulatory specifications concerning "edible meat offal" and "lard and other rendered pig fat." The Lisbon treaty that took the place of the rejected EU constitution doesn't supply this want of happiness. The UN's Universal Declaration of Human Rights does state, in Article 24, that "Everyone has the right to rest and leisure, including . . . periodic holidays with pay." Leave it to UN delegates to expect to be paid for their freedom. Anyway, a holiday is not the same as the pursuit of happiness, as anyone knows who's spent a holiday dragging whiney children on a tour of UN headquarters.

The New Testament, arguably the founding text of Western civilization, mentions happiness just seven times and never in a happy context. Peter's First Epistle, to persecuted Christians in Asia Minor, says, "if ye suffer for righteousness' sake, happy are ye." Jesus is quoted as using the word "happy" only once, on the occasion of washing his disciples' feet. We admire the Son of Man but we sons of a gun who populate America do not pursue our happiness in this manner.

The United States is the first—and so far only—among happy nations. "Happy the people whose annals are blank in history books," wrote Thomas Carlyle. Just ask Americans a question about American history, watch them draw a blank, and you'll see that we are the happy people indeed.

Not that Americans seem very happy at the moment. And maybe Americans never have seemed happy. In his 1741 sermon "Sinners in the Hands of an Angry God," Jonathan Edwards doesn't sound as if he's talking to a cheery crowd.

> The God that holds you over the pit of Hell, much as one
> holds a spider, or some loathsome insect, over the fire, ab-
> hors you . . . he looks upon you as worthy of nothing else,
> but to be cast into the fire.

And now, due to the financial crisis, the mortgage foreclo-
sure crisis, and health care reform, we're not only going to hell,
we're broke, homeless, and sick while we're waiting to get in.

Happiness, like the freedom we're so happy to have, is
elusive—slippery in physical and conceptual grasp. "I'm happy"
doesn't mean "I'm having fun." Remember all the fun you've
had. When it was really fun it didn't end up making anybody
very happy. "I'm happy" is distinct from those spasms of ecstasy
that do not elicit any coherent phrases. "I'm happy" is more or
less equivalent to "I'm content," which means "I won't complain because nobody listens to me."

"Happy" is often used as a none too complimentary modi-
fier: "happy-go-lucky," "slaphappy," "happy horseshit," "happy
as a pig in same." The catchphrases "one big happy family," "Is
everybody happy?," and "I hope you're happy now" are never
spoken without a happy smirk of irony. Then there's whatever
John Lennon was getting at with "Happiness Is a Warm Gun."
Although it's true under certain circumstances. Try defend-
ing the perimeter of your outpost in Kandahar by squeezing a
puppy.

However, it should be noted that the Declaration of Independence reads, "Life, Liberty, and the Pursuit of Happiness,"
not, "Life, Liberty, and Whoopee." Jefferson's choosing "the
pursuit of" rather than plain "happiness" is a reminder of what
happens to the poor suckers who, in their pursuit of happiness,
catch the thing. America's legions of minor, temporary tabloid
stars can tell the rest of the story, if they survive their stardom.

Happiness is hard to attain, harder to maintain, and hardest
of all to recognize. Pick the time of your life when you know you
were happiest. You didn't know how happy you were at the time.
When the kids were little and you hadn't slept in three years.

That first job in Manhattan, being groped by the assistant marketing director and sharing a one-bedroom Avenue X and Millionth Street apartment with eleven other people. Those halcyon days at college that you flunked out of.

Old people are forever reminiscing happily about all sorts of things that wouldn't seem conducive to happiness, such as World War II. Will the forsaken recipients of largesse from bilked charities someday wax nostalgic about Bernie Madoff's avuncular ways? The fact that we don't know when we are happy raises the disturbing possibility that you and I are wildly happy right now. I hope my wife doesn't find out.

What's happiness doing in the Declaration of Independence anyway? The original phrase is "Lives, Liberties and Estates," a brief catalog of man's inherent rights that appears several times in John Locke's *Second Treatise of Government*. Locke was one of the Enlightenment's foremost proponents of natural law and the rights it naturally bestows, rights that are so much a part of our nature nothing can take them away, and we can't get rid of them. There were other important natural law theorists, such as Hugo Grotius, Samuel von Pufendorf, Jean-Jacques Burlamaqui. America's patriotic thinkers relied mostly on Locke because he argued the case for people's right to dissolve their government. Also, he was easier to spell. When Thomas Jefferson drafted the Declaration of Independence he was referring directly to chapter IX of the *Second Treatise,* where Locke says that men are "willing to joyn in Society . . . for the mutual *Preservation* of their Lives, Liberties, and Estates, which I call by the general name *Property*." Every educated person understood the reference (moral philosophy not yet having been replaced by civics in the educational curriculum). Many educated persons must have wondered about Jefferson's substitution of laughs for land.

The fact that property wasn't mentioned in the Declaration of Independence still seems odd. The French revolution's Declaration of the Rights of Man lists property second only to liberty, and the French revolutionaries had less respect for other people's property (and less property) than did the signers of the Declaration of Independence.

Jefferson may have been trying to convey the idea that our new nation wasn't going to be a European kind of place. America wouldn't be parceled into aristocratic estates kept intact by primogeniture and entail. Entail is a legal restriction on property, usually land, limiting its inheritance to linear descendants of the owner, and primogeniture is a further restriction that leaves out the girls in the family. Entail was necessary to preserve the power (formerly military, later economic) of the holders of the titles of nobility, which titles the U.S. Constitution would soon ban.

Entail was in bad odor in the late eighteenth and early nineteenth centuries. Rationalist thinkers of the day were ashamed of inherited class distinctions even (sometimes especially) if they were so distinguished. Entailed estates were considered to be the ground from which grew the twisted family tree of peerage occupied by the serpent who urged the rotten fruit of birthright upon Edenic mankind. The metaphor is overfertilized, perhaps, but, said Tom Paine in *Common Sense,* "Original sin and hereditary succession are parallels. Dishonorable rank! inglorious connection!"

Nowadays, when the British royal family is mostly blogfare and titled Frogs and Wops are of no interest to anyone but *Vanity Fair* editors, we wonder at the fuss over entail. Yet in the late 1700s Georgia went so far as to pass a law against such laws, attempting to keep the privileged few from monopolizing the broad cotton fields of Tara. Never mind that for every free household in Georgia the state had approximately thirteen thousand acres of unpopulated land. (And Scarlett O'Hara's father was a bog Irish upstart who won the joint in a poker game.)

More than a decade after America had declared its unentailed independence and made pretensions of nobility illegal, Jefferson was still railing against transgenerational claims on property. In a letter to James Madison, he wrote *"the earth belongs in usufruct to the living."*[3] The italics are Jefferson's and "usufruct" is the legal right to use and enjoy something—pursue happiness with it—during one's lifetime. Tom Paine would make the point again in his 1791 pamphlet *Rights of Man*: "Man has no property in man; neither has any generation a property in the generations that are to follow." Even Jane Austen would comment on the issue. In *Pride and Prejudice* she has the silly Mrs. Bennet say, of the rule that decrees precisely who inherits what, "There is no knowing how estates will go once they come to be entailed."[4] (A remark that advocates of various environmental and conservationist entails upon land might want to ponder.)

All these proponents of liberty versus heredity were taking their cue from Adam Smith in *The Wealth of Nations*, published, appropriately enough, in 1776. Smith wrote that the laws of entail "are founded upon the most absurd of all suppositions, the supposition that every successive generation of men have not an equal right to the earth, and to all that it possesses."[5]

---

3. Paris, September 6, 1789.
4. Chapter 13.
5. Book III, chapter 2.

America as a place for fresh starts has illustrious intellectual credentials. Not that we'd know it by looking at America's uncouth frontiersmen, woebegone backwoods pioneers, seedy homesteaders, giddy forty-niners, illiterate cowboys, huddled masses of immigrants, and Internet start-up wingnuts.

"Pursuit of Happiness" also may have supplanted "Property" in the Declaration of Independence because of definitional concerns. Locke died in 1704, when "Estates, which I call by the general Name *Property*" was still synonymous with land and land was still synonymous with riches. Until Adam Smith succeeded in improving the world's understanding of economics (if he ever did), land was considered to be the only ultimate source of profit.

The Declaration was written by Thomas Jefferson but it was revised and edited by John Adams and Benjamin Franklin. Jefferson was a devotee of property in the sense of land and chattel (of animal and other kinds). But Adams, although a farmer, had no Jeffersonian vision of America as a pure, agrarian society. Perhaps this was because Adams, unlike Jefferson, made a living from his farm. Adams and Franklin understood that trade, manufacture, and finance would be as significant in America as "real" estate. And Franklin had a personal interest in a type of ownership different from a land title, ownership of what we would come to call intellectual property. (It was not coincidental to Franklin's influence that the power to approve patent rights would be granted in Article I of the forthcoming Constitution, and that the first act passed by the new Congress of the United States would concern patent law.)

Jefferson was often concerned about money, but Franklin and Adams were actually thinking about it. Still, we can

understand why, for reasons of popularity and taste, the rights
in the Declaration of Independence aren't listed as "Life, Liberty, and Stinking Wealth."

Roger Pilon, chief constitutional scholar at the libertarian Cato
Institute, in Washington, D.C., believes there was another reason
that property rights were handled with delicacy in the Declaration of Independence. Pilon concludes that Jefferson detected a
flaw in the logic of Locke's "unalienable" rights. Property has to
be alienable, in a legal sense, or you can't sell it. If we lived in a
country where property was unalienable, Steve Jobs and Steve
Wozniak would still have the pocket calculator that they sold to
raise the money to start Apple. Therefore when we go to work
there's nothing on the screen of the computer that doesn't exist
at the job we don't have because we're still farming the twenty-
acre tobacco patch that our ancestors gypped the Indians out of
for beads and trinkets the last time anybody was allowed to buy
anything, in the reign of George III.

Property is an important aspect of the pursuit of happiness. Pilon says the founding fathers would have considered
this materialistic side of happiness to be, as the founding fathers liked to say, self-evident. Try paying your mortgage with a
hug. (Though that's what the U.S. government is helping some
people do these days.)

The authors of the Declaration of Independence, the Constitution, the *Federalist Papers,* and the other sources of the
American idea of freedom had a materialistic philosophy of independence. And they knew enough philosophy to know that
they did. Jefferson, Franklin, Adams, Hamilton, Madison et al.
did not believe that American independence was the same as

the independence preached by the so-called cynic philosophers of ancient Greece. The cynics held that independence lay in individual "autarchy" or rigid self-sufficiency. Diogenes was said to have been elated to discover he could drink from his cupped hands and dispense with his mug. But this shows that even the most ascetic pursuit of happiness involves consideration of the material world. (And it shows that Diogenes was a dope who had to found a whole school of philosophy to figure out how to get a puddle to his face.) Diogenes lived in a barrel. "*Whose* barrel?" Jefferson, Franklin, and Adams would have asked. There was nothing cynical about America's founding fathers, in any sense of the word, but nothing naive either.

Pilon maintains that "Pursuit of Happiness" replaced "Property" in the Declaration of Independence not to denigrate material wealth but to expand the idea of materialism. America was established as a way for Americans to make and do things. What sort of things Americans make and do and whether these things lead to great riches, pious satisfactions, or transitory pleasures is nobody's business but our own. America's political institutions are supposed to be the machinery for our making and doing. America is a tool. America is the only place on earth or in history created in order to be both free and teleological. Teleology is the idea that phenomena are guided by a purpose. America is. But—and here's what's new—we Americans get to individually, personally, separately decide on any purpose we want.

What's the point of other nations? It's something of a historical mystery. Conquering the world seems to be a purpose for some nations—fortunately not too many, and fortunately not too often, and most fortunately they always fail. Maybe nations arise to provide their citizens with mutual protection against external and internal threats. If this were the usual case, world history would read like an account of the interrelations of the cantons of Switzerland. Certain nations seem to exist strictly to torment their neighbors or their citizens or both. Other nations are simply . . . there. Notice how in Paris people go to cafés and just sit around all day being French. Or, if they prefer to sit around all night, they can be Spanish and not have dinner until 11 p.m. A friend of mine once said about the rural Turks that they're so lazy they get up at four in the morning to have more time to do nothing. It gives an American the heebie-jeebies. We have to be making and doing. Albeit what we make is often a mess. And what we do is often our undoing. Lately we've added being to making and doing. What Americans are being is famous or infamous (there's no longer a distinction) or fabulous or centered or self-actualized or spiritual or eco-conscious or, frequently, real fat. Anyway, we Americans are very, very busy, and we owe it all to three little words in our Declaration of Independence.

Or maybe that's wrong. Maybe Jefferson, Franklin, and Adams were just happy. Jefferson was famously uxorious. Perhaps his wife, Martha, slipped up to Philadelphia for a dirty weekend. And Franklin landed the Declaration of Independence printing contract. And Adams was working his way through a cask of Madeira. The Declaration's first draft might have read, "Pursuit of Nookie and Graft and I'll drink to That." If it had gone to press this way we'd be a different people, less busy and less happy and more inclined to say such things to each other as "Wealthy Birthday!," "Drunken days are here again!," and "Sexually aroused to meet you."

4

The Happy Realization
That All Freedoms Are
Economic Freedoms

(And Failure Is an Option)

The free market is the greatest repository of our freedoms. Economic freedom is the freedom we exercise most often and to the greatest extent. Freedom of speech is important—if you have anything to say. I've checked the Internet; nobody does. Freedom of belief is important—if you believe in anything. I've watched reality TV and I can't believe it. Freedom of assembly is important—if you're going to an assembly. Most people are going to the mall. And, at the mall, they exercise economic freedom.

We have the cow of economic freedom. Do we take the cow to market and trade her for the magic beans of bailout and stimulus? When we climb that beanstalk we're going to find a giant government at the top. Are we going to be as lucky as Jack the giant killer was? I'm not sure Jack himself was that lucky with his giant killing. That's Jack's version. My guess is that Jack spent years being investigated by giant subcommittees and now Jack's paying a giant tax on his beanstalk bonus.

The free market is not a creed or an ideology that political conservatives, libertarians, and Ayn Rand acolytes want Americans to take on faith. The free market is simply a measurement. The free market tells us what people are willing to pay for a given thing at a given moment. That's all the free market does. The free market is a bathroom scale. We may not like what we see when we step on the bathroom scale, but we can't pass a law making ourselves weigh 165. Liberals and leftists think we can.

The free market gives us only one piece of information, but it's important information. We ignore it at our peril, the way the leaders of the old Soviet bloc did. They lost the cold war not just because of troops or tanks or Star Wars missile shields. Even Reagan and Thatcher couldn't win the cold war by themselves. They needed allies. And the allies were Bulgarian blue jeans. The Soviets lost the cold war because of Bulgarian blue jeans. The free market was attempting to inform the Kremlin that Bulgarian blue jeans didn't fit, were ugly and ill-made, and nobody wanted them at any price. People wouldn't wear Bulgarian blue jeans—literally not to save their lives. But the Kremlin didn't listen. And the Berlin Wall came down.

It is with some diffidence that I write about economic matters. I was an English major or, as people in business call it, stupid. The best investment I've made lately? I left a twenty-dollar bill in the pocket of my tweed jacket last spring and I just found it. But I do know enough to thank business for existing.

Business investment defines humanity. Animals don't invest. If a dog has a surplus he will eat it all and vomit it up rather than give a portion of it to another dog in return for shares in car chasing or the chewing of shoes.

Business investment defines civilization. Barbarians don't raise money through debt and equity. They raise money through stealing. (Although, during the boom in subprime mortgage lending it was sometimes difficult to tell the difference.)

Nonetheless business investment is one of the most important ideas in history. If it weren't for business investment all the inventors, innovators, manufacturers, wholesalers, and retailers who have brought prosperity to the modern world would have to get their money the way the rest of us do, by asking their wives.

The free market is the greatest repository of our freedoms, but the free market is dead. It was killed by the Bolshevik revolution, fascist central planning, Keynesianism, the Great Depression, World War II economic controls, the British Labour Party victory of 1945, Keynesianism again, the Arab oil embargo, Bill Clinton's and Tony Blair's "third way" economics, and the 2008 financial crisis. The free market died at least ten times in the past century.

And every time the free market expires there is, for some reason, a flurry of renewed interest in Adam Smith. Smith preached the gospel of the free market. Economic well-being—the wealth of nations, as it were—depends solely on freedom. There is, first, the freedom to choose our method and means of economic employment, what Smith indicated by his "division of labor." Second is the freedom to exchange the products of our labor for the products of other people's. Smith championed the abolition of restraints and monopolies on commerce, a doctrine that came to be known as "free trade." Third, there is the freedom to decide what it is we want to accomplish with our labors and trades. Smith termed it people's "regard to their own interest." This is sometimes called "pursuit of self-interest." Jefferson's more felicitous phrase is, of course, "pursuit of happiness." Anyway, when the freedom of the free market leads to screwups, people always want to know what Adam Smith would say about "market failure." It's a "Hello, God, how's my atheism going?" moment.

Adam Smith would be laughing too hard to say anything. Smith spotted the exact cause of the 2008 financial meltdown not just before it happened but 232 years before, probably a record for advice to sell short. In Book II, chapter 1 of *The Wealth of Nations,* Smith wrote, "A dwelling-house, as such, contributes nothing to the revenue of its inhabitant . . . If it is to be let to a tenant for rent, as the house itself can produce nothing, the tenant must always pay the rent out of some other revenue." Smith therefore concluded that, although a house can make money for its owner if it's rented, "the revenue of the whole body of the people can never be in the smallest degree increased by it." Bingo. Subprime mortgage collapse.

Smith was familiar with rampant speculation, or "overtrading," as he politely called it. The Mississippi Scheme and the South Sea Bubble had both collapsed in 1720, three years before his birth. In 1772, while Smith was writing *The Wealth of Nations,* a bank run occurred in Scotland. Only three of Edinburgh's thirty private banks survived. The reaction of the

Scottish overtraders to the ensuing credit freeze sounds familiar. "The banks, they seem to have thought," Smith said, "were in honor bound to supply the deficiency, and to supply them with all the capital which they wanted to trade with."[6]

According to Smith, the phenomenon of speculative excess has less to do with free markets than with high profits. "When the profits of trade happen to be greater than ordinary," he said, "overtrading becomes a general error."[7] And rate of profit, Smith claimed, "is always highest in the countries that are going fastest to ruin."[8] Judging by how America invested in 2007 and voted in 2008 that would be us.

The South Sea Bubble, offering shares in a government monopoly on trade with the Orient, was the result of machinations by Britain's lord treasurer Robert Harley, earl of Oxford, who was looking to fund the national budget deficit. The Mississippi Scheme, with securities backed by France's land claims in North America, was started for the same reason by the French regent Philippe, duc d'Orléans, who gave control of the royal bank to Scottish financier John Law, the Charles Ponzi of his day. And the 2008 crisis was the product of interest rate manipulations by the Federal Reserve Bank under its chairman Alan Greenspan, for the same reason yet again.

John Law's fellow Scots, who were more inclined to favor market freedoms than the English let alone the French, had already heard Law's plan for "establishing a bank . . . which he seems to have imagined, might issue paper to the amount of the

6. *The Wealth of Nations*, Book II, chapter 2.
7. *The Wealth of Nations*, Book IV, chapter 1.
8. *The Wealth of Nations*, Book I, chapter 11, conclusion.

whole value of all the lands in the country." The parliament of Scotland, Smith noted, "did not think proper to adopt it."[9]

A single misconception allows overtrading folly to turn into speculative disaster, whether the overtrading involves commercial monopoly, Louisiana wilderness, tulip bulbs, dot-com stocks, or home mortgages. The misconception is that unlimited expansion of prosperity can be created by unlimited expansion of credit.

Wild flights of borrowing can be effected only with what Smith called "the Daedalian wings of paper money."[10] To produce enough of this paper requires either government or something able to put the arm on government the way modern financial institutions can. They are too _____ (pick your adjective) to fail. The U.S. government likes to peddle its powers. Financiers like to shop their influence. Smith pointed out, "The government of an exclusive company of merchants, is, perhaps, the worst of all governments."[11]

Business people are innately no better than other people. Some may be as bad as politicians. But the political power of government is required to let business people do their worst. Given that power, it's easy.

The plan that Adam Smith put forth for creating prosperity is more complicated. It involves all the baffling intricacies of human liberty. Smith proposed the frighteningly complex program of everybody being free—free of bondage and of political,

---

9. *The Wealth of Nations,* Book II, chapter 2.

10. *The Wealth of Nations,* Book II, chapter 2.

11. *The Wealth of Nations,* Book IV, chapter 7.

economic, and regulatory oppression. Smith once told a learned society in Edinburgh that "Little else is requisite to carry a state to the highest degree of opulence but peace, easy taxes, and a tolerable administration of justice."[12]

With Smith's clear understanding of political inclinations in matters of adjudication, exaction, and war, we can guess the tone of sarcasm in which he spoke.

How would Adam Smith fix a mess such as the current recessionary aftermath of financial collapse? Sorry, but it's fixed already. The answer to a decline in the value of speculative assets is to pay less for them. Job done.

We could pump the banks full of our national treasure. But, Smith said, "To attempt to increase the wealth of any country, either by introducing or by detaining in it an unnecessary quantity of gold and silver, is as absurd as it would be to attempt to increase the good cheer of private families, by obliging them to keep an unnecessary number of kitchen utensils."[13]

We could send in the experts to manage financial institutions. But, Smith said, "I have never known much good done by those who affect to trade for the public good."[14]

And we could nationalize our economy. But, Smith said, "The state cannot be very great of which the sovereign has lei-

12. Dugald Stewart, *Collected Works*, vol. 10, *Biographical Memoirs of Adam Smith et al.*

13. *The Wealth of Nations*, Book IV, chapter 1.

14. *The Wealth of Nations*, Book IV, chapter 2.

sure to carry on the trade of a wine merchant or apothecary."[15]
Or run General Motors.

Opposition to the free market is forever expressed in outrage at
capitalist success. Capitalism exploits workers, robs widows and
orphans, and concentrates wealth in the hands of the rapacious
few. Speaking as a capitalist, if only. Critics of the free market
think of capitalists as being Donald Trump and the faceless, and
therefore even more wicked, partners at Goldman Sachs. Were it
true that the free market did nothing but breed flocks of Donald
Trumps and packs of Wall Street grab-alls, it wouldn't be just
the left that's out to get them. The rest of us would be hunting
them for sport. But that's not all the free market does, that's not
who capitalists are, and capitalism is by no means a product of
the free market anyway.

To undertake a material project—whether it's a Great Pyra-
mid of Khufu, an Atlantic City casino, a hospital for widows
and orphans, or a papier-mâché Gandhi puppet for the annual
Peace Pageant at the Waldorf School—requires a fund of accu-
mulated resources of some kind, no matter if it's just paste and
recycled paper. This is capital.

Capital can come from savings. Capital can come from bor-
rowings. Capital can come from consideration given in return
for proportionate ownership of the project in hand. Capital can
come from paper money that a central bank has pulled out of its
ass. Kings, republics, communist dictatorships, Microsoft, the
Salvation Army, and Somali pirates all need capital, and they
all discover ways to obtain it. Capitalism, so called, is when free

---

15. *The Wealth of Nations*, Book V, chapter 2.

people accumulate capital of their own free will for use on freely determined projects.

The fact of the matter is that most of these projects flop. Donald Trump, for example. Every property he touches seems to go to hell. "Fat Cat" would be the wrong epithet for Trump. If someone other than paroled former Enron accountants were keeping his books, he'd probably be shown to have a net worth less than that of your twenty-pound tabby who just shredded the drapes.

What's good about the free market is that it allows capitalism to—so to speak—trump success. The free market lets capitalism fail. Think of all the wonderful moneymaking ideas people get—and you've probably had some of these ideas yourself: chocolate-covered hairballs to give your feline something yummy to cough up; a line of bottled water for dogs with flavors such as "Puddle," "Pond Scum," and "Toilet Bowl"; plastic garbage bags that solve the annoying which-side's-up? problem by being open on both ends; scented candles for men— "Mandles"—that fill a guy's home with smells of "Pool Hall," "Old Dog," "Gear Oil," "Beer," and "Frying Meat"; home colonoscopy kits; and FunScreen to protect children from dangerous exposure to fun. Use FPF 40 if the kid has a skateboard.

In a free market, people (notably my stock broker) invest money in these things and in businesses such as a chain of restaurants run by Wolfgang Puck's younger, dumber brother, Hockey; an Orthodox Jewish Wilderness Outfitter whose guides specialize in catching gefilte fish on dry flies; a way to cash in on recession thrift with a day-old sushi bar; low-cost off-season foliage tours of New England featuring bus trips through Vermont in March; and a deal to mitigate the effects of both the mortgage lending crisis and climate change by buying all the

Sub-Zero freezers from foreclosed McMansions and renting them as affordable housing to Polar Bears.

Imagine a world where all such schemes come to fruition. You've just imagined a cross between North Korea and Dubai. And you've just explained where those Bulgarian blue jeans came from.

Bad ideas can also happen in democratic societies where the full range of freedoms, including the freedom to fail, are presumed to exist. At the end of 2008 and the beginning of 2009 America conducted an economic intervention that kept businesses that were staggering around, intoxicated by overtrading, and blinded by MBA moonshine from falling down the manhole of liquidation.

The business of government is failure-proof. Social Security finances have, over the past thirty years, arrived at a condition that would make the most hardened trader of collateralized debt obligations blanch. America is on the verge of having a huge surplus of retirees. Government subsidies produce surpluses because subsidies always produce surpluses, the way they did with America's subsidized wheat and cheese. Subsidized surpluses, their prices fixed by law, do not respond to the usual methods ("Absolutely Final Going Out of Politics Sale!") of clearing markets. What will we do with all the old people? We may have to—as we did with the wheat and cheese—donate them overseas in hope of aiding developing countries that lack age, wisdom, and the Early Bird Special at Denny's.

Fortunately most of America is still allowed to fail. Economic failure, however, harms good business as well as bad. The arrogant and greedy come a cropper, but so do the innovators and visionaries. And this is fine too.

Per the Adam Smith analogy, Icarus, with youth's ready affinity for new technology, sees all sorts of possibilities in flight. These elude his earth-oriented, sandal-tech father Daedalus, who just wants to get out of Crete. Icarus takes off on his own. He experiences the thrill of a soaring venture, briefly becomes a hot property, gets his wings singed, has a meltdown, and undergoes a rapid decline in personal fortune.

So it went with the Internet bubble, and so it had gone before with the railroads. Trains are another example of a visionary innovation that suffered a valuable fizzle. Railroad building was vital to America's business expansion. But speculation in railroad stock offerings in the 1870s led to a dot-com of a crash. Good as railroads are, what if every proposed railroad had succeeded? Do we want a railbed in the driveway? Would it be convenient to take the train into the McDonald's drive-through lane? It's probably no coincidence that, shortly after the railroad bust, the automobile was invented.

A too visionary adoption of innovation can be disruptive, as the residents of Nagasaki could attest. Private developers of an atomic bomb would have realized that the device has detrimental side effects and exposes investors to numerous class-action lawsuits. Venture capital for the Manhattan Project would have dried up.

If, for instance, the Segway had been introduced in the visionary, innovative late 1990s, we'd be up to our handlebars in the things. Segways would be whizzing along our sidewalks, caroming off baby carriages, causing havoc among dog walkers, squashing the sleeping homeless, and forcing joggers to run for their lives. Teenage boys, with youth's ready affinity for new technology, would hotrod the Segway. "Mall racing" would ensue with grisly accidents and loss of life or, anyway, toes. Congressional hearings

would be held. The National Highway Traffic Safety Administration would get involved. Airbags, shoulder restraints, and "stand
belts" would be mandated plus two extra wheels to ensure stabil-
ity. The Segway, by now, would be a car.

As it is, the Segway was introduced in the more cautious
and pragmatic early 2000s. Thus the Segway had a chance to
prove itself on its own merits and become gradually integrated
with the social fabric as a useful device for making law enforcement officers look ridiculous.

The free market teaches us a lesson in the value of failure. And,
after all, it is not just the growth of an economy that depends on
failure. So does the growth of a democracy.

In America, unlike, say, Zimbabwe, the political system is
based on politicians being losers. John Quincy Adams swiped
the White House from Andrew Jackson in 1824. Jackson had
fought duels and Indians and the British, but Old Hickory
chose to wait for a metaphorical bloodbath in 1828 rather than
start a real one. Nor did the combative lawyer Samuel J. Tilden
stoop to battle the crooked ascendancy of Rutherford B. Hayes
in 1876. And after the Florida recount imbroglio of 2000 Al
Gore conceded gracefully. More or less.

Only once—following the election of Abraham Lincoln in
1860—did prominent American politicians refuse to accept the
blessings of failure. They started the Civil War, a terrible failure
that's kept our nation free and united ever since.

To failure we owe our form of government, and also our actual,
physical form. Death was biology's greatest invention. Without

death there's no you. I just keep dividing into endless replications, the whole bunch of myselves forging a lifestyle truly open to the criticism of being "all about me."

Failure is obviously the key to Darwinian selection. Survival of the fittest can't work if the unfit are still hanging around. There they go, dodging comet collisions, being chased by predators but always managing to escape, getting stuck in tar pits then extraditing themselves somehow, getting tar all over the place. It drives the fittest mad.

Failure is necessary to evolution but equally necessary to creationism. Picture Adam and Eve, after an eternity, all talked out, with the thrill of nudity long expired. Adam keeps mowing and dethatching and reseeding paradise. He's given up golf. He doesn't have the swear words for it. He futzes, putting the billionth coat of Thompson's Water Seal on the fence around the Tree of Knowledge. Eve redecorates Eden. It's Olympus this eon, Valhalla the next, then a modern, minimalist Nirvana. She changes all the names for the animals and stares at the fig tree, hoping for something new and stunning in this year's leaf. The beasts of the field are tired of one another. The lion lies down with the lamb; the lamb snores. The serpent ends up eating all the apples himself. He's too fat to go out and do any tempting. From this we're supposed to fill a Bible?

It seems unfair that failure is essential to every aspect of freedom —economic freedom, political freedom, the freedom of existence itself. But freedom is not fair. Much can be made of the fact, I suppose. Personally, I'm immune to the complaint. I have a twelve-year-old daughter, Muffin. All I hear is, "It's not fair! It's not fair! It's not fair!"

I say to her, "Honey, you're cute. That's not fair. You're smart. That's not fair. You were born in the United States of America. *That's* not fair. Darling, you had better get down on your knees and pray to God that things don't start getting fair for you."

5

The Murderous Perverted Nuptial Bliss Method of Establishing Political Principles

We can formulate some powerful, free, and responsible ideas about government if we keep "Kill Fuck Marry" in mind.

But first, to clear the ideological air, let's confess that there are no conspiracies that rule the world. There's no universe-mastering cabal of capitalists, communists, Islamic fundamentalists, International Monetary Fund executives, Federal Reserve Bank governors, New World Order functionaries with their UN black helicopters, Trilateral Commission initiates, Freemasons, Bavarian Illuminati, Rosicrucians, Knights Templar, Mafia families, Chinese triads, Mexican drug gangs, Jesuits, or Google. And no, no, no, no, it's not the Jews. They'd do a better job.

The presidential "Birther," the 9/11 "Truther," the JFK assassination "Grassy Knoller," and every other conspiracy buff is announcing aloud: "The world is so stupid that even I can understand it."[16]

---

16. But good news for Birthers! While the nativity of the current chief executive may have occurred in Hawaii or in Kenya or away in

All conspiracy theories are based on the assumptions that, first, any group of people numbering two or more can agree on anything for longer than it takes to get another beer from the refrigerator and, second, that they'll keep their mouths shut. People are so liable to tell secrets that if, for example, people don't have any embarrassing secrets to tell about themselves, they'll make up some. No motivation is sufficient to induce mankind to be effectively secretive. The minute we have a secret we make a Tiger Woods of ourselves.

Then there are the supposed unconscious, involuntary, or automatic conspiracies that history engages us in, such as the Marxist class struggle. It's over. The social class known as assholes won. The inevitabilities of dialectical materialism, of the march of progress, of globalization, the Internet, Francis Fukuyama's *End of History,* and even climate change are fictions after the fact. This is not to say they aren't true. It's just to say that, with a little imagination, anyone can explain the course of human events from the minutest cause to the grandest effect: for want of a nail the shoe is lost, for want of a shoe the horse is lost, for want of a horse the rider is lost, for want of something to fill *Poor Richard's Almanac* a proverb is swiped from seventeenth-century metaphysical poet George Herbert, and—for want of a better idea—Benjamin Franklin's resulting prosperity and social prominence leads to independence for the thirteen American colonies.

There are always groups of people upon whom to blame things: the Flemish if you're a Walloon, the Walloons if you're Flemish, both of them and the rest of the dorks in Brussels if

---

a manger, no crib for his bed, here are eight presidents who *definitely* weren't born in the United States of America: George Washington, John Adams, Thomas Jefferson, James Madison, James Monroe, John Quincy Adams, Andrew Jackson, and William Henry Harrison.

you're an EU citizen. But there's no group of people upon whom to blame *everything*, except in a free and democratic society where we can, with confidence, blame everything on ourselves.

And what about ourselves? We're individuals—unique, disparate, and willful, as anyone raising a houseful of little individuals knows. And not one of these children has ever written a letter to Santa Claus saying, "Please bring me and a bunch of kids I don't know a pony and we'll share."

The great religions regard us as individuals, treating sin and salvation as individual matters, at least most of the time. There are occasional group discounts, such as with the Sixth Commandment. Thou shalt not kill—unless you all get together and attack the Canaanites. We Christians don't say our prayers as if we were responding to random polling of the likely blessed with a plus or minus five percent margin of error on "Thy will be done." Buddhists don't have a graduated meditation rate that shifts the burden of enlightenment to those with greater assets in the sitter department. And Allah doesn't welcome believers into paradise saying, "You weren't a good Muslim, but you were standing in a crowd of good Muslims when you detonated the explosives in your suicide vest."

Virtue is famously lonesome, and vice is pretty solitary for some of us too. We experience pain and pleasure individually, which is what showed President Clinton to be such a pigeon plucker when he told us he "felt our pain." We forgave him because we were spared feeling his icky pleasures.

Making a statement of individuality is not the same as professing a philosophy of "individualism" with loud cries of "Me first!" Individuality is, like the free market, a measurement, not a moral argument. Individuals are the units we come in. Basing a political system on something other than individuals—communes, collectives, identity groups, Twitter-generated flash mobs, Grateful Dead followers still wondering where the heck to go—isn't wrong, it's stupid. It's like having a counting system that goes: few, less, some, more, none. Even within a family people have to be treated as individuals, otherwise we stuff a tampon up Dad, give Mom a table saw for Valentine's Day, and turn the toddler loose on the rider mower.

Therefore, if we were inventing a new political system . . . Stop. We do *not* want to invent new political systems. Whenever people tell you they are going to wipe the slate clean, it's your slate they mean to wipe. The political systems that we have already are plenty bad enough. Newly invented political systems mean Mussolini, Hitler, Franco, Lenin, Mao, Pol Pot, or, at best, Che Guevara—best because the Bolivians killed him before he caused any trouble.

Political systems cannot be treated as if they were blueprints from Habitat for Humanity, drawn to a conscious plan and given a fixed start date. The social engineering involved in political subdevelopments such as these leads to bodies buried in the basement. Nor were existing political systems created intentionally, for reasons bad or good. There is a notion that somewhere in a dusty archive or dog-eared poli-sci textbook there's something called a "social contract." It was mentioned first by Thomas Hobbes in the seventeenth century, then by John Locke, and later by Jean-Jacques Rousseau. Hobbes thought that man had surrendered liberties to government in return for order and safety. Locke thought that man had volunteered powers to government in return for safety and order. And Rousseau thought . . . he thought all sorts of things. He was French.

Just where and when did hairy apemen come down from trees and speak to the fine points of this agreement before speech was invented? Who decided how many ughs would be in the Gruntstitution? Few? Less? Some? More? None?

The rule of political systems is that we must play the hand we're dealt lest we be shuffled and discarded. Or this would be the rule of political systems if it weren't for the fact that 230-odd years ago some hicks sat down in a flea barn in a no-account burg in what might as well have been Borneo and invented a new political system that's been the envy and astonishment of the world ever since.

We know nothing about where political systems come from. We don't even know where they don't come from. And considering the shiftless, slave-trading, bed-hopping, debt-ducking (and that's just Thomas Jefferson) nature of America's founding fathers, who also included rum-soaked bunkum merchants and Indian-massacring land swindlers (and they all oppressed women and weren't vegans) we should be careful about saying that certain societies or nationalities or religious persuasions aren't "ready for democracy."

As I was saying, if we were inventing a new political system, the first question should be, "What is good for everyone?" By everyone we ought to mean everyone as in *every one*. The question can't be, "What is good for one?" That's monomaniacal and results in a political system like the New Hampshire presidential primary. The question can't be, "What is good for someone?" Everything's good for *someone*. The New Hampshire presidential primary is good for someone who owns a Motel 6 in Keene, New Hampshire. The question can't even be, "What's good for almost everyone?" or "everyone who matters?" or "the majority of everyone who gives a shit?" Political systems always end up asking these questions. The place where things end can't be the place to begin. (Unless politics is as much like a Monopoly board as leftists say it is.) Finally, the question can't be, "What is good for everyone as a whole?" There is no whole. Individuals are available only individually. A complete set cannot be collected, even by force.

No matter how newly inventive we're being with our political system we should take a few lessons from the past. The philosopher George Santayana told us that when we ignore history we're doomed to repeat it, and, if high school is anything to go by, the same is true for civics.[17]

Mankind has made improvements in living conditions over the past couple of million years. (Some people don't think so. To those people I say: dentistry.) The improvements that have been good for everyone are those that have increased the dignity of the individual—have given the individual broader scope, greater self-accountability, and more authority over everything in the world (except other individuals who have the authority to tell the first individual to butt out).

Judaism provided individuals with one God and one law before whom all men are equal regardless of wealth or rank. Christianity pointed out that every individual has precious intrinsic worth, even the most lowly among us such as those we vote for in the New Hampshire presidential primary. The

---

17. Santayana managed to ignore World War II. He was in Rome when the conflict broke out. He moved into an Italian convent and stayed there until his demise in 1952. (What Santayana was doing in the Italian convent we don't know. But he wasn't killed and he wasn't married to death.)

growth of trade and private enterprise let individuals acquire autonomy and material goods by means other than delving in muck and killing each other. And the industrial revolution allowed millions—now billions—of individuals to lead a housed, clothed, and fed life. (Albeit with some unfortunate side effects such as those polar bears living in our Sub-Zero freezers.)

So there we have it, a political system that consists entirely of us individuals, each of us entirely free. All that we free individuals have to do now is ask each other, "What do we want?"

And be told to shut up. There's no way to learn the infinite wants of myriad individuals, and why are we so nosy anyhow?

Yet we do know some things that we want from a political system, whether we care to know or not. What we want, from even the freest political system, is relief from freedom. Freedom is not a tranquil condition, witness all the killing, fucking, and marrying involved. We want order and safety, per Hobbes and Locke. That is, we want the police, the army, and TSA to be on the lookout (for *other* people, thank you). But we also want somewhere to turn when our weather, our economy, our health, our luck, or ourself screws up.

Some people cannot enjoy the benefits of freedom without assistance from their fellows. This may be a temporary condition, such as childhood and when I say I can drive home from the bar at 3 a.m. just fine. Or, due to infirmity or affliction, the condition may be permanent. Aid must be given. Assets must be redistributed.

All political systems are redistributive. The most rigidly individualistic political theorist can't get away from redistribution. The theorist might wish he could invoke the "fuck you" clause in the Kill Fuck Marry paradigm when it comes to poor people. But there are always more poor people than political theorists. The poor people may go for the kill.

Also there's the sympathy, compassion, and basic human decency embedded deep within our souls. Embedded so deep that they're often invisible and sometimes impossible to find. But we won't admit that. We may not have a conscience, but we do have something inside that keeps us from announcing that we don't. This something may be, again, the fear that everyone will kill us.

Political systems are redistributive because every political system is modeled to some extent on the original political system, the family, that hotbed of communism. Within a family the dictum of Marx is valid: "From each according to his abilities, to each according to his needs." But the family is not a good model for a political system. For one thing Marxism ceases to work when it is extended outside the family by even so much as the factor of one bum brother-in-law. For another thing, think about your family. Or, worse, think about mine. Talk about kill, fuck, marry. There are branches of my family too looney even for jobs in government. Now imagine that my family occupies hundreds of thousands of square miles and is made up of tens of millions of people too looney even for jobs in government. It's California.

On the other hand, what's a better model for a political system than the family? The coral reef is okay, as long as we don't have to go anywhere. Animal farm has been tried. Facebook would be weird.

In the makeup of a halfway decent political system, the quality of freedom (including the free market), the quantity of individuality, and the fact of redistribution are fair assumptions, I assume. Redistribution is where the political fun begins. How much? Of what? To whom? By which means? And where the hell do we get it from?

This is the crux of the liberal versus conservative argument in modern democracies. Let us say that the argument is "Does size matter?" and that liberals and conservatives are bickering about the amount of redistribution to be done. This isn't quite true but it's close enough for government work. Let us say further—liars though we may be—that both the left and the right mean well and that each wants "what is good for everyone." Redistribution still causes a huge fight. People are never going to agree about it. The quarrel will go on forever.

And let's hope it does. An end to the argument would be horrible. The moment when we're all in accord about every social benefit with which we all will be provided forever is the moment when we enter my twelve-year-old daughter Muffin's alternate universe where "everything is fair." You don't want to go there. Pink blasting on the iPod speakers. The laptop glowing with snarky BFF e-mails. The stinking hamster cage. The huge polyester tangle of the abandoned My Little Pony collection. Floors a fathom deep in wadded-up Aéropostale outfits, tattered *Twilight* books, fruit roll-ups and half-chewed gum. There are snits. There are sulks. There is bitter sarcasm apropos of nothing. And you'd better hope you're not a younger sister. For younger sisters life really is hell where "everything is fair."

A few nonpartisan (or, at least, not very political) observations can be made about redistribution. When any authority of any kind undertakes to redistribute goods and services we can be sure we'll be told that "what goes to the poor" has "come from the rich." Those who are indignant at the rich say so; the indignant rich do too. But who's rich? You are. To someone who lives in the slums of Karachi you're rich. I don't care if you're driving a 1990 Geo Tracker, haven't had a job since Cher was a babe, and your trailer home just burned down because your wife's boyfriend's meth lab exploded, you're rich. You're farting through silk as far as that person in Karachi who's *looking* for a job as a suicide bomber is concerned. Accusing someone of being rich is like accusing someone of adultery in the Gospel of St. John. Let he who is without anything anybody wants cast the first vote.

We all praise the virtue of sharing, but perform the following thought experiment about the sharing process. Imagine that your family is matched, by lot, with five other families and that the resulting half dozen familial units must pool their resources and come to mutual decisions about how those resources are to be allocated. For a brief moment that sounds like an intriguing combination of reality TV and the 1960s. Then we recall what an awful combination reality TV and the 1960s would have been. *The Real Housewives of Charlie Manson.*

Since we've already determined that you're rich, let's institute a requirement that the other five families be poorer than yours. And why is a small bad idea like this supposed to get better if you make it bigger? It stinks in your hometown. How is it going to smell nationwide?

Nor does the idea improve if you shrink it. How small would that pool of resource sharers need to be to make it practical, sane, and unstupid? Even within our immediate families we don't share our resources fairly (as Muffin is totally fond of pointing out). And in most families collective decision making doesn't rise above the level of hamster purchase. (My dogs favor having the hamster—with a side of fries.)

What if the shared resource pool is restricted to only a married couple? Surprise divorce filing! And your spouse's lawyer just called to say you're rich.

Another rule of redistribution can be extrapolated from a family circle: Never do anything to (or for) a stranger that you wouldn't do to (or for) your bum brother-in-law. (I'd like to note here that I have a perfectly respectable set of brothers-in-law: an engineer, an industrial designer, a medical researcher, and a deceased career military man. So it's *your* bum brother-in-law we're talking about.)

You can't let your sister and her five kids by six different fathers starve, but you can try to make her husband get a job. And you can (at least in my state) run him off at gunpoint if he beats her.

Or say your brother-in-law isn't a bad guy, just drunk and crazy and high on drugs. He's living on the street and talking to people who don't exist. Do you pick him up by his collar and belt, heave him in the back of your car, and get him some help? Or do you respect his civil rights and let him freeze in doorways and get run over by a bus? Yeah, I'm for the bus myself. But you know the kind of fit your sister is going to pitch at the funeral, screaming and yelling, and that will get your mom started and you'll never hear the end of it.

We're in the same situation, politically, as we are with our sister. We have to help. But when an overcollectivized political system is allowed to make all the decisions about who gets help we end up helping some people who are hardly helpless. Maybe they're worthy people whom we love dearly but we still don't feel obligated to share our resources with them.

For instance, there you are, scraping along, three kids in school, and the house worth half what it was a few years ago. And your dad needs a knee replacement. Let's say your dad, oh, served three terms in Congress and then went to work as a Washington lobbyist so that his net worth is, um, a couple hundred million dollars. Do you pay for the knee operation? What's the old fart still doing out on the tennis court anyway? And will somebody tell me why the goddamned hell Medicare isn't means-tested?

Redistribution is practiced in every democratic political system (and allegedly practiced in most of the systems that aren't democratic). This is well and good as long as we're mindful that, a lot of the time, redistribution works about as much as your brother-in-law.

Power, freedom, and responsibility are the main features of our politics. We pay with our freedoms to relieve ourselves of our responsibilities, and this is how others get their power over us.

Maybe a nicer way to put it is, "We come together in a political system to share the burden of our responsibilities." Except that's bullshit. We snatch the material resources that constitute freedom from everywhere and everyone we can. We're such thieves of freedom that we pick our own pockets. And we turn these resources over to politicians so power mad they're willing to endure the filth of politics to gain the least bit of mastery over their fellows.

If we do our stealing for the sake of Hobbesean order and safety, we're not much to blame. But a look at government expenditure indicates that safety and order aren't our first concerns. According to the 2009 federal budget we're spending $651.2 billion on defense and $26.6 billion on administration of justice. Add to this the $91.8 billion that we spend, quite rightly, on veterans' benefits and we get a total of $769.6 billion in Hobbesian diminishments of our freedom—two and a half thousand dollars or so apiece and worth it, or we hope so. But in the same year we're spending $694.8 billion on Social Security; $420.1 billion on Medicare; $316.8 billion on the other government-funded health care services; $54.2 billion on "income security" including unemployment, disability, and welfare benefits; $12.2 billion on social services providing vocational education and training; $22.6 billion on the agricultural subsidies that everyone wants to kill; and $38.3 billion on humanitarian foreign aid. That's one and a half trillion—a lot of giving. We're giving until it hurts. That is, we're giving until it hurts *other people*, since we're giving more than we've got.

Do we need to employ the untrustworthy and rapacious power of government to effect the redistribution that our political system requires? We'll never know. We're too busy running up to our untrustworthy government leaders and thrusting gifts of additional rapacious power upon them so that we don't have to take care of Grandma. She doesn't know who we are anymore and she smells. Even if Hobbes and Locke had been talking crap and there never was such a thing as an internal or external threat to society, people would still form governments just to shirk responsibility. It's "Kill Fuck Marry" again. In our political heart of hearts we're all twenty-two, rich, and beautiful. We fuck all we want, then we get an abortion or ask the National Institutes of Health to kill the HIV virus, and if we do get married it's just for a couple of months. (Don't forget the prenup!)

6

The Purgatory of Freedom and the Hell of Politics

The best way to have a good political system is to avoid politics. But political disengagement deprives us of opportunities for bitching at politicians and pushing them around. This is occasionally useful and always a pleasure. In our democracy we don't get in trouble by trying to make politicians mad. We get in trouble by trying to make them like us. Our political system goes to hell when we want it to give us things.

There are certain things we may reasonably demand of our political system, of course. But most of these things are negative rights. And often it's the political system itself that's violating those rights. The most sensible request we make of government is not "Do something!" but "Quit it!"

As for our positive rights and the goodies we expect to gain with them, we're confusing politics with Halloween. Politicians don't mind. They love devising programs of incentives and disincentives for the populace. Trick or treat! And a ghouls and goblins political system is fine for those among us who are really scary. But, for the rest of us, don't be surprised if we go house to house—White House to House of Representatives to Senate—and, ringing doorbells as furiously as we may, get nothing but healthy fruit.

If there's something we want, politics shouldn't be our first resort. Politics is all taking, no making. Whatever politics provides for us will be obtained from other people. Those people won't love us.

And we don't love them. When we gain our ends through political takings it's because of a certain bad idea. What we're thinking leads to death, destruction, and taxes. What we're thinking is that we live in a zero-sum world: there is a fixed amount of the things I want, and when anybody has anything I want they've taken it from me. If you get too many slices of pizza, I have to eat the Domino's box.

This is a particularly poisonous idea because for most of history it was true. There may have been a prehistorical moment when all we had to do to get more mammoth meat was walk over the next hill and avail ourselves of some unpopulated spot such as Europe. But civilization is based on land for grazing and crops. There's only so much land. If I'm on it, you're off. That's the world's shortest history of warfare, and probably also the history of class conflict, serfdom, slavery, nationalism, racism, and genocide.

Zero-sum thinking is a name for envy. Ovid, in his *Metamorphoses*, gives an apt description of the "House of Envy" (as a poet in that most zero-sum of political systems, the Roman empire, might): "Envy within, busy at the meal of snake's flesh . . . her tongue dripped venom. Only the sight of suffering could bring a smile to her lips. She never knew the comfort of sleep, but . . . looked with dismay on men's good fortune . . . She could hardly refrain from weeping when she saw no cause for tears." I didn't know Hillary Clinton's involvement in politics dated back to the reign of Augustus.

Then one day the idea of zero-sum wasn't true. We see its falsehood being revealed by population growth during the late Middle Ages in Europe and India and China (with time-outs for Black Death, massacring invasions, and the Thirty Years' War). The industrial revolution would further this population trend, but the original human anti-Malthusianism doesn't seem to have been the result of science or invention. Adam Smith thought the cause was simple expansion of trade, giving farmers a motive to grow more food than was needed just for eating, reseeding, and the rats.

By now there shouldn't be a zero-sum thought left in our heads. We should be free of all of zero-sum's begrudgings. We know we can make more of everything. Energy, to name one. When did our vital supply of lamp-lighting whale oil run out? We didn't notice because we were too busy inventing kerosene and electricity.

Once again India and China (Europe not so much) are showing the way with the vast expansions of their economies. We can bake more pizza (or naan, as the case may be). We can clone more cows. We can raise more plants (under grow lights in the closets of our off-campus apartments). There's even additional beachfront property on its way, thanks to climate change and seaside development in Greenland. Celebrity offers the ultimate disproof of zero-sum. The amount of celebrity was always limited by the need for something to celebrate. Click through your cable channels. Not now.

But there is one field of endeavor where zero-sum remains the awful truth: politics. Even in the most free and democratic country politics is about power. There's a fixed quantity of power because there's a fixed quantity of me. Power you have over me is power I lose to you. And political power is different from other power because political systems are different from other social systems. A political system has the legal monopoly on deadly force. We're all involved in a variety of social systems, such as that bunch of social snobs with their system of blackballing us at the country club. They're allowed to ban us from the tees but they aren't allowed to pick us off with sniper fire from their clubhouse bar. Governments can. Nothing sums up zero-sum like death.

Because government is zero-sum there aren't two congressmen wedging their fat butts into the same seat in the House of Representatives. We don't have 300 million Supreme Court justices telling nine old Washington shysters in black bathrobes whether they'll get a lawyer at Gitmo. The chiefs of the Joint Chiefs of Staff aren't all commander-in-chiefs commanding "Forward March!" to one another until they collide in a group hug.

Political power is awful, and power is awful anyway. Lord Acton, one of nineteenth-century Britain's great defenders of liberty, wrote, "Power tends to corrupt, and absolute power corrupts absolutely." This was in a letter to Anglican Bishop Mandell Creighton,[18] and the subject was papal infallibility (something Acton, a devout Catholic, argued against at the First Vatican Council). Sure, and if power can do the likes of that to the Holy Father in Rome, just think what it's done to Harry Reid.

We have to be careful about giving power to people—for their own sake, among every other reason. We won't get our power back easily. And when we try to get our power back it

18. Acton, *Essays on Freedom and Power,* Boston, 1948.

isn't pretty: Washington at Valley Forge, Paris during the Reign of Terror, the czar's family in Yekaterinburg.

Nonetheless we are continually tempted to confer power on government—to delegate our power (as some would have it), to alienate our power (as Jefferson would have been more likely to say). And it's not only a desire to escape from our responsibilities that tempts us. The American government is a huge tool, a formidable engine, mighty in its operation and nearly irresistible in its movement (never mind that it doesn't know where it's going). The temptation is to use a tool like this when something needs fixing. Whether the tool suits the task isn't a question we always ask ourselves, as those of us who received Home Depot gift certificates for Father's Day can attest. Maybe we shouldn't change the battery in our wristwatch with the electric drill. But what if it's a cordless DeWalt with a 3/8" chuck and fifty different bits?

Or, to put the case differently, the government is a rottweiler ready to be unleashed on your problems. And you've stuffed raw meat down the front of your pants.

One method of being careful with government power is to think about our messy government the way we think about our messy personal lives. There are furious ex-spouses, bitter former lovers, and various outstanding child support judgments. We don't want too much of this in one place, which is why we moved to Phoenix.

America's founding fathers knew enough about messy personal lives to make sure that the chief concerns of the Constitutional Convention were a federalist decentralization of power and a system by which each branch of government would check the other branches of government and balance their power with power of its own. What if all the ex-spouses, former lovers, and kids whose school fees we're supposed to be paying become friends and get the same lawyer? America's founding fathers would have rather moved to Phoenix than let this happen.

It is a good idea for as much government power as possible to be distributed to the smallest possible units of government—the cities, towns, townships, and counties that are scattered all over the United States plus those scattered states themselves. John Sununu, former governor of New Hampshire and chief of staff to President George H. W. Bush, is a cantankerous and truthful man. He's also an engineer. He compares reliance on local government to a goal of mechanical engineering: short control loops. The hot and cold faucets in your shower are a short control loop. If, instead of being located in the shower stall, those hot and cold faucets were in the basement, that would be a long control loop. This is not to say that a short control loop always works. You may be out of hot water. But it's better to stand in the shower fiddling with a useless faucet than to march naked and dripping through the house, amazing the children and shocking the cleaning lady, down two flights of stairs into the grungy basement, and fiddle with a useless faucet there. If our neighbor on the local sewer commission votes to raise our sewer rates, we can go next door and yell at him or stuff a potato up the tailpipe of his car. Stuffing a potato up the tailpipe of the limousine of the president of the United States is a federal crime, or they'll make it one if we try.

Despite the clear and evident sense of the short control loop argument we are deaf to it. When something's wrong we don't consult the sewer commissioner next door, even if what's wrong is backed-up sewage. We go straight to Washington and, bypassing even the House and the Senate, expect the president himself to take time off from trying to get his limo started and come over to our house with a plunger.

We do this not just because we're morons but because federal government in the United States is more efficient, less corrupt, and harder-working than state and local governments. Illinois. Say no more.

The federal government attracts the biggest talents in administration, legislation, jurisprudence, and bureaucracy. And those talents are exercised under the greatest scrutiny because the news media pay attention to the federal government. All this makes for a good thing. Of its kind. In the shark tank the juiciest bait attracts the biggest sharks. If that juicy bait happens to be something interesting, such as we the drowning taxpayers, attention will be paid.

The only effective way to keep power decentralized is by making sure our society provides ungovernmental ways of being powerful. The biggest talents should be offered bait in places other than Washington. Let the good and the great flounce around in the arts, spout pious bilge from pulpits, fill the minds of the young with drivel at great universities, spread patronizing smarm through charitable organizations, and rob all comers in business. Just one ready, necessary thing is needed to set the hook in this lure of decentralization. Thank God for money. And whenever we meet a rich person, however loathsome, we should be sure to say, "Thanks! The disgusting fact of your existence helps spread the manure of life around and keeps it from piling up in one spot, under the Capitol dome."

Political power, however, remains the most powerful of powers, so people will continue to be drawn to it. What kind of people

we know too well. The politician's personality has been bril-
liantly described.

> A pervasive pattern of grandiosity (in fantasy or behav-
> ior), need for admiration . . . beginning by early adulthood
> . . . as indicated by five (or more) of the following:
>
> (1) has grandiose sense of self-importance (e.g., exaggerates
>   achievements and talents, expects to be recognized as su-
>   perior without commensurate achievements)
> (2) is preoccupied with fantasies of unlimited success, power,
>   brilliance
> (3) believes that he or she is "special" and unique and can only
>   be understood by, or should associate with, other special or
>   high-status people (or institutions)
> (4) requires excessive admiration
> (5) has a sense of entitlement, i.e., unreasonable expectations
>   of especially favorable treatment or automatic compliance
>   with his or her expectations
> (6) is interpersonally exploitative, i.e., takes advantage of oth-
>   ers to achieve his or her ends
> (7) lacks empathy: is unwilling to recognize or identify with
>   the feelings and needs of others
> (8) is often envious of others or believes that others are envi-
>   ous of him or her
> (9) shows arrogant, haughty behaviors or attitudes

The authors of the above passage had no idea they were writing about politics. They thought they were writing about mental
illness. This perceptive analysis of politicians appears on page 717
of the American Psychiatric Association's *Diagnostic and Statistical*

Manual of Medical Disorders, fourth edition, under the heading "Diagnostic Criteria for Narcissistic Personality Disorder."

The only thing in the shrinks' notes that might seem odd to a voter is "lack of empathy." Every politician is always telling us how much sympathy, understanding, and fellowship he or she has with us and how deeply he or she is moved by our hopes, our dreams, and our fears. About such too muchness of protestation, Hamlet's mother—no mean politician herself—has an oft-quoted line.

There is an enormously powerful machine that with one wrong turn can kill us all and it's being run by crazy people. What are the chances this will turn out well?

In the meantime it's costing us a fortune. Milton and Rose Friedman, in their seminal[19] work about liberty and market freedoms, *Free to Choose,* showed why government is so expensive. The Friedmans devised what in logic is called a "truth table" to show that there are, logically, only four categories of spending. The table looks like this.

		ON WHOM SPENT	
		You	Someone Else
WHOSE	Yours	I	II
MONEY	Someone Else's	III	IV

19. "Seminal" is such a PBS word, as close as PBS comes to talking dirty. And *Free to Choose* was indeed a companion piece to a 1980 PBS special by the same name. The dirt, in this case, could be heard thumping on the lid of the Carter presidency's coffin. Jimmy Carter must have realized that when, as a liberal Democrat, even public broadcasting turns on you, you're dead as a smelt.

Category I is you spending your money on yourself. Let's take cars as an example of something to spend on and me as an example of someone doing the spending. I have a splendid Porsche 911 that I got a great deal on, buying it almost new from a dentist who scared himself and bought a Lexus Coupe instead. When you spend your money on yourself you get—as nearly as you can—exactly what you want and you bargain as hard as you can for it.

In *Category II*, when you're spending your money on someone else, you still bargain hard. But you're not quite as concerned about getting exactly what's wanted. Although I'm sure my wife is very fond of the Kia Rondo minivan I purchased for her and the kids. And it was a lucky break for me that it had been sitting on the dealer's lot for almost a year because it is a somewhat unfortunate shade of orangey green.

You spend someone else's money on yourself in *Category III,* and I'm on the fence between the Aston Martin DBS coupe that goes for close to $300,000 and letting "someone else" off easy with an Alfa Romeo 8C Competizione spider convertible, a steal at $230,000.

With *Category IV* you're not involved at all. It's not your money and nothing's in it for you. So it might as well be billions spent on jack shit or, as the government called it, "cash for clunkers."

There is only one problem with the above examples from the Friedmans' truth table. The Friedmans assume that the person doing the four categories of spending is not an insane evil pig. Can that assumption be made about me if I'm a politician? Things don't look good even in *Category I.* That 911 is a relic of my footloose bachelor days. I've had it for twenty years and could never afford another one. Unless I plunder the children's college fund.

For *Category II* I'll stick with the orangey-green Kia. My wife had a couple glasses of wine last night, and it turns out she hates it, I mean *hates* it.

In *Category III* I'm pulling out the stops with a $2 million Bugatti Veyron—the fastest production car in the world—*and* a $500,000 Maybach 62 that has plenty of room in the back for all the booze, drugs, and strippers that someone else's money can buy.

But it's *Category IV,* the category into which all government spending falls, where crazy, malicious hoggishness can be given full play. If I'm buying a car for you peons, it may not be enough for me to just throw money away on something you don't want. I may have other thoughts. Maybe I think I'd prefer a world that isn't full of smelly pollution and where I don't have to worry about the temperature getting so high that I'll be able to bake bread by leaving dough outdoors on an August day in Nome. So your car has to be an even more unfortunate shade of green than my wife's Kia. Plus I don't like being stuck in traffic or constantly looking for parking places. So your car not only shouldn't emit greenhouse gases, it shouldn't do anything else. Plus don't forget I hate your guts because I'm an insane evil pig. Thus no research, development, or manufacturing expense will be spared to provide each one of you with . . . a hybrid Yugo.

There are very few excuses for allowing goods and services to be allocated by political means unless you're trying to get something that isn't yours. And what you get is a Yugo. That's one Yugo for you versus innumerable reasons for the rest of us to prevent you from allocating goods and services by political means. Make that innumerable plus three.

1. Concentrated benefits and diffuse costs.
2. Invisible opportunities.
3. Committee Brain.

One of the things that allows us to be eaten up by our politics is that we are eaten very slowly, one political bug bite at a time. If we were being eaten by a boa constrictor or Kim Jong Il we'd notice. But in a democracy it takes years for us to wake up and say, as Ronald Reagan so memorably said in the 1942 movie *Kings Row,* "Where's the rest of me?" Not until almost forty years later, when Reagan was running for president, did we taxpayers finally come to our senses and ask the same question about our paychecks.

The first secret of our obliviousness to being swallowed is what's called "diffuse costs." A government idiocy may be expensive, but the expense is spread so broadly that none of us feels the nip of that expense very hard. For instance, let's take a government idiocy that's quite expensive and, furthermore, obviously and evidently useless to the nation, and which doesn't even have any political support. Joe Biden. Joe Biden costs us $227,300 a year in salary plus $90,000 for official entertainment expenses. (O'Doul's, because somebody has to keep a clear head during those White House Beer Summits.) Then there are the tens of thousands spent on around-the-clock White House staffers trying to keep Joe Biden's mouth shut and more tens of thousands for shoe shines, black neckties, and Air Force 2 fuel when unimportant foreign leaders die, and at least $20 worth of Secret Service protection. We'll round it off and take a guess and say that Joe Biden costs us $600,000 a year. But there are 300 million of us. Yes, Joe is a complete waste of two-tenths of a cent, but who cares?

Libraries NI
Omagh Library
1 Spillar's Place
Omagh
BT78 1HL
Tel 028 8244 0733

Borrowed Items 06/11/2017 11:49
XXXXXX5901

Title	Due Date
't vote! : it just ourages the bastards	27/11/2017

nk you for using this unit

r Library Doesn't End Here
free eBooks and Audiobooks
ww.librariesni.org.uk
sk staff for details

Joe does. That is the "concentrated benefits" part of "concentrated benefits and diffuse costs." The two-tenths of a cent means nothing to us, but it's everything in the world to Joe Biden who will bear any burden, meet any hardship, pay any price (well, no, *we'll* pay the price), even go on Bill O'Reilly to remain one and a half heartbeats from the presidency. (The half a heartbeat is the time it will take Nancy Pelosi to wring his neck and become president herself.) And so it goes with other government idiocies even more expensive than Joe such as AIG and Homeland Security.

The expense of politics wouldn't matter so much if it weren't for the opportunities that are destroyed by this spending. Money that's poured down rat holes can't be used to pay the Pied Piper. (Not that the government of Hamelin town *did* pay the Pied Piper.) These destroyed opportunities—or "opportunity costs," as economists call them—are the flip side of zero-sum. It is a source of wickedness to believe that the world contains a fixed amount of resources. Paradoxically, it is a source of wickedness to forget that the world *does* contain a fixed amount of resources, *at any given moment.* The amount of resources is infinitely expandable, but in order to expand it we have to spend the resources we currently have on something other than Joe Biden.

Because our opportunities are lost—so lost they never got anywhere near us—it's easy and maybe comforting to forget about them. These opportunities are certainly invisible to politicians. They don't see the businesses that weren't started, the innovations that weren't pursued, the charitable donations that weren't made, and the beer I didn't drink because a jerk professor and a college-town cop (talk about a fight I don't have a dog in) drank it in the White House backyard.

Meanwhile politicians work themselves into a lather of rationalization about the benefits of government spending. In this they are aided by the more vile kinds of economists such as Paul Krugman and the late John Kenneth Galbraith. Using liberal political-economic reasoning I can prove ... *anything*. I can prove that shooting convenience-store clerks stimulates the economy.

Jobs are created in the high-paying domestic manufacturing sector at gun and ammunition factories. Additional emergency medical technicians, security guards, health care providers, and morticians are hired. The unemployment rate is lowered as job seekers fill new openings on convenience-store night shifts. And money stolen from convenience-store cash registers stimulates the economy where stimulus is most needed, in low-income neighborhoods where the people who shoot convenience-store clerks go to buy their crack. I am simply flabbergasted that the Democratic majority in the House and Senate isn't smoking crack and shooting convenience-store clerks this very minute, considering all the good it does.

And where are the missing opportunities? There were some convenience-store clerks who thought they were going to have an opportunity to do something, if only grab a smoke outside the back door on their break. But they're dead.

The expense of politics is bad, the political destruction of opportunities is very bad, but nothing is as dreadful as the brain of a politician. Ha. Ha. Ha. What brain? Alas, it's worse than a joke.

Taken one by one, politicians are of dull-normal intelligence. They're not Stephen Hawking, but they're not Mark Sanford either, except Mark Sanford. But when you put politicians together in governments you get committees. In Congress they even come right out and call the committees committees.

We've all been on committees. We know what happens to intelligence and common sense when a person becomes a committee member—*Committee Brain.*

You live in a neighborhood with a playground. The kids in the neighborhood would like to play tetherball but the playground has no tetherball pole. A committee is formed to raise funds for tetherball: Committee to Raise Funds for Tetherball, CRFT.

CRFT is started by a group of pleasant, enthusiastic, public-spirited neighbors. The minute any of these neighbors becomes a member of CRFT he or she will begin to express his or her pleasant, enthusiastic public spirit by turning into one of the following:

The Fanatic

Everyone loves tetherball! Everyone will donate to CRFT! There are a lot of rich people in the neighborhood! They'll all donate! Let's set our fund-raising goal at one million dollars! I'll "throw in" (prolonged giggling) five bucks to "get the ball rolling"!

The Martinet

We have to draw up a charter and form a nonprofit corporation with a chairman, a president, vice president, secretary, treasurer, development officer, human resources executive, four calling birds, three French hens, two turtle doves, and a partridge on a tetherball pole exactly ten feet high. We're talking about *regulation* tetherball, played according to North American Amateur Tetherball Association rules.

The Dog in the Manger

We need to get permission from the County Zoning Board, the City Council, the Parks Department, and adjacent landowners who may complain about tetherball noise. That part of the playground is too damp for tetherball. It might be federally protected wetlands. We can't do any fund-raising without advertising. We can't advertise without raising funds. The kids would rather have a tennis court.

The Person Who Is Stupid Even by Committee Brain Standards

So the rope, like, has a ball on it?

The Worrier

Padded pole, breakaway tether, a lightweight foam ball, and ban on playing after dark or when visibility is poor and when the sun is shining, to avoid UV ray skin cancer damage. The kids should wear helmets and kneepads and safety belts.

The Person with Ideas

If we call ourselves the "Committee to Raise *American* Funds for Tetherball—*Yeah!*" we can use the acronym CRAFTY. Let's set up a challenge grant to erect a second tetherball pole in the inner city. "Midnight Tetherball" could be an alternative to crime for deprived youth. We can also promote tetherball as a way to combat child obesity, which would make us eligible for funding from United Way, and we should also apply to the Gates Foundation. Or invent a tetherball cell phone app and rake in the cash. We'll have a tetherball league—no, three—Adults, Juniors, and Tether Tots. This could be a great Title IX thing. If our daughters are varsity-level tetherball players they'll get into Yale. I'll go on the Internet and check out tetherball coaching. I'll bet the best coaches come from eastern Europe. We could probably hire the top coach in Bucharest for peanuts if we get him a green card. And from there it's straight to the Olympics!

The Person with Ideas, None of Which Has Anything to Do with Tetherball

Is the tether biodegradable? Is the pole made from recycled materials? Many playground balls are manufactured in third world countries using exploitative child labor. Let's be sure to utilize organic fertilizer and indigenous plant species when seeding the tetherball play area. Power mowers will contribute to climate change.

The Bossy Person

Who says the same thing as everyone else on the committee but louder.

The Person Who Won't Shut Up

Who says the same thing as everyone else on the committee but more often.

The Person Who Won't Show Up

Unless his or her vote is crucial, in which case he or she shows up and votes the wrong way.

You

You actually do all the work and call forty people and ask them each to donate $10, and half of them do, and you raise the $200 needed, only to find out you need $200,000 because the House of Representatives' Economic and Educational Opportunities Committee's Select Committee on Opportunities in Physical Education's Subcommittee on Americans with Disabilities Act Compliance has delivered a report to the House/Senate Joint Economic Committee, which has referred legislation to House and Senate conference committees to reconcile a bill requiring all tetherballs to be wheelchair-accessible no matter how high the tetherballs fly in the air.

Given the complete dominance of politics by Committee Brain, the wonder is that anything gets done, and the horror is that it does. What government accomplishes is what you'd expect from a committee. "A camel is a horse designed by a committee" is a saying that couldn't be more wrong. A camel is a seeing-eye dog designed by a committee and available free with government grants to the halt and the lame.

Yet committees are ancient and ubiquitous in our civilization. Moses goes to a business conference with God and the next thing you know, Exodus 32:1, "the people gathered themselves together." And someone says, "All in favor of worshipping a golden calf . . ."

Same thing in the Roman Senate: "All in favor of relinquishing power to Caesar, then stabbing him . . ."

And again in the boardrooms of Lehman Brothers, Merrill Lynch, and Fannie Mae: "All in favor of investing in loans to people who made loans to people who made loans to people with houses that aren't worth pissing on if they catch fire . . ."

Committees persist although their decisions are invariably stupid. Therefore committees must provide some value to our civilization with their stupidity. And they do. In fact it could be suggested that our freedoms find their surest protection in stupidity.

We owe the thought to Lord Brougham, another of nineteenth-century Britain's great defenders of liberty. As a Member of Parliament, Brougham carried the bill to make slave trading a felony in 1810 and was instrumental in passing the Reform Bill of 1832 that widely expanded the electorate and made seats in Parliament more nearly representational. Brougham (who, incidentally, had a style of fancy carriage named after him, set the fashion for going to the Riviera, and became himself quite stupid later in life) said, "All we see about us, Kings, Lords, and Commons, the whole machinery of the State, all the apparatus of the system, and its varied workings, end in simply bringing twelve good men into a box."[20]

In other words, what makes and keeps us free is a committee— the jury. Governments have the legal monopoly on deadly force, and, in a free country, the thing that prevents the government from forcing us into prison or onto the lethal injection gurney any time it likes is the need for a jury verdict. Our government cannot inflict any punishment or penalty upon us unless what we have done is so obviously wrong and outrageously bad that even a feebleminded, asinine, obtuse, muddled, stubborn, and silly committee, which never agrees on anything, agrees.

Stupidity is our unwavering safeguard. And one that, it is to be hoped, will protect Joe Biden when he's arrested for shooting convenience-store clerks.

---

20. "Present State of the Law," 1828.

7

Morality in Politics

And What's It Doing in There?

Morality is important to politics. Important is not the same as necessary. You can remove morality from politics like you can remove the head from a chicken and they'll both keep going, politics much longer than the chicken. Politics will continue to run around, flap, and spurt blood forever without its morality.

What's important about morality in politics is us. We own the chicken farm. We must give our bird-brained, feather-headed politicians morals. Politicians love to think of themselves as "free-range" but they do not have the capacity to hunt or gather morals in the wild. If we fail to supply them with morality, politicians begin to act very scary in the barnyard. These are enormous headless chickens and they have nukes.

But, while we all say it would be good if politicians were moral, we all get a little nervous when morality in politics is advocated. We worry about the separation of church and state. We are afraid that "morality" is the thick end of whatever is the opposite of a wedge and that this tool will be used to knock church and state back together with a bang that will result in, at best, the Taliban and the Spanish Inquisition, if not Sarah Palin.

None of these is a good idea. Yet separation of church and state is a problem that's well addressed by the First Amendment. We should be demanding separation of state and coven.

Maybe politics is inherently evil. Maybe politics is so evil that anything we do for it, even attempting to supply it with morality, just feeds the beast. I trust this isn't true but I can't say the thought doesn't trouble me.

The sum and substance of politics was expressed in the 1860s by prescient Russian radical Nikolay Chernyshevsky: "Man is god to man."[21] The faith of politics is in the holy goodness and correctness of mankind (as soon as humanity gets politically corrected) and in the collective mystical solidarity of that reformed mankind. These impious sentiments were nicely put by the poetic genius—and political idiot—Percy Bysshe Shelley.

> *Man, one harmonious soul of many a soul,*
> *Whose nature is his own divine control*[22]

Making man divine takes some doing. But there have been numerous volunteers for the task, starting, predictably, with a French philosopher. Claude Adrien Helvétius (1715–71) made the awful pronouncement that "It is . . . only by good laws that

---

21. Cited in *The Russian Revolution*, Richard Pipes, New York, 1990.
22. *Prometheus Unbound* (1820), Act IV.

we can form virtuous minds."[23] This notion was taken up with enthusiasm by Marx and Engels in the *Communist Manisfesto*.

> You must, therefore, confess that by "individual" you mean no other person than the bourgeois ... This person must, indeed, be swept out of the way, and made impossible.[24]

Then the idea was put into force by the likes of Leon Trotsky who, writing in 1924, sounds more full of romantic crap than Shelley.

> Man will become incomparably stronger, wiser, subtler. His body will become more harmonious, his movements more rhythmic, his voice more melodious.[25]

If he lives.

Thus the virtuous "new man" imagined by politics comes to rule over heaven and earth. Call him "Ben." Or call him "Jerry." He rewrites Genesis so that Adam loses all of his ribs, and half his backbone, to ensure that the Garden of Eden is fully representative of the spectrum of human sexuality. Endangered species go first into the ark. (Now, how do we get those brontosaurs out of the vegetable garden?) Moses is called to the mountaintop to receive the Ten Thousand Nice Ideas urging the Israelites to be "in touch with their feelings" and deploring speech that's "hurtful and divisive." Joshua blows his horn and the residents

---

23. *De l'Esprit, or Essays on the Mind,* London, 1819.

24. Part II: "Proletarians and Communists."

25. Quoted in *A Concise History of the Russian Revolution,* Richard Pipes, New York, 1995.

of Jericho join in on recorders and tambourines. There's no capital punishment in the Judea of Pontius Pilate, Jesus does three to five in imperial minimum security. He writes *The Gospel of Prison Reform* and starts a socially conscious, sustainable small business by using his heavenly powers to invent refrigeration. The symbol of universal salvation is ice cream. We are blessed with an infinite number of cleverly named delicious flavors. But we are required by law to use someone else's tongue to lick them.

Politics violates not only the first commandment about who's God, it violates the other nine as well. Politics could hardly function without bearing false witness. Likewise, without taking the Lord's name in vain. The more so given that, in politics, the Lord who is so loosely sworn by is you and me—mankind.

In modern government politics has taken the place of mere tyranny. The result has been more killing in the past century than in all the preceding centuries combined. Covetousness and stealing define redistributive politics, and, without redistribution, politics would have no political support. And graven image is as good a way as any to describe the fiat money by which redistributive politics operates.

Politics' insistence upon involvement in every human activity, twenty-four hours a day, seven days a week, is more anti-Sabbatarian than golf. The Social Security system is no way to honor thy father and mother. As for adultery, there was, and there may still be, Bill Clinton.

Even to be "politically engaged and informed" may make us one of the devil's party, driving around town with a "Vote Satan" bumper sticker. Listen carefully to that most politically engaged and informed radio network NPR and hear the evident relish with which it reports misfortune, inequity, and suffering around the world. The unspoken gleeful message is, "More occasions for more politics!" Nor are conservatives without delight in others' misery. How we long for unemployment, anxiety, anger, and fear of bombs in boxer shorts on the next election day.

I believe in original sin, and politics may be its name. However, unlike some of my fellow Republicans, I do not believe God is involved in politics. Observe politics in America. Observe politics around the world. Observe politics down through history. Does it *look* like God is involved? When it comes to being a political activist, that would be the Other Fellow.

This said, unless we intend to climb the pillar of Simeon Stylites and evict Simeon or go off the grid with a one-man militia in the Bitterroot Range or otherwise isolate ourselves from every arrangement among persons—even the Dalai Lama hasn't been able to manage it—we need another way to approach morality in politics.

Morality is a larger sphere than politics—thank goodness, literally. The relationship between things that are moral and things that are political can be shown with Venn diagrams. This is a method invented by British logician John Venn[26] to illustrate the categorical propositions of logic. Here, for example, is a Venn diagram of the categorical proposition known as "universal negative":

26. If Professor Venn had had any idea how his diagrams would be used in PowerPoint presentations, he would have shot himself, but not before tracking down Professor Pie, inventor of the pie chart, and shooting him first.

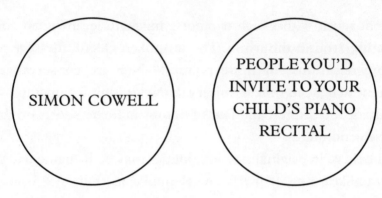

And here is a Venn diagram of politics and morality illus-
trating the categorical proposition known as "particular affir-
mative," which can otherwise be stated as "most politicians will
burn in hell:"

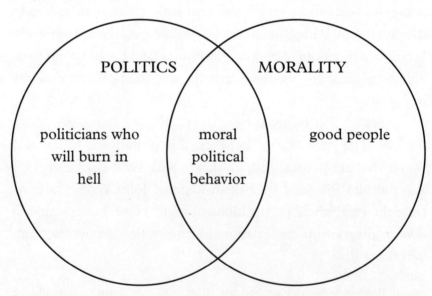

If the circle of politicians fell completely within the circle of morality, none of us bitchmongers in the media would
have a job. Fat chance of that. Even if a miracle happened and

politicians and voters became saints, there are aspects of politics that fall outside morality.

There's no perfectly ethical way to conduct taxation or utterly good method of exercising public domain. Some injustice in letting the guilty out of jail must be preferred in our legal system to the greater injustice of jailing me. Then there's war. The reasons for a war may be highly principled. The conduct of a war can not be.

And religion doesn't work. Even the most religious among us shouldn't get ourselves so sanctimoniously confused that we think religion and morality are identical. It's not a one-circle Venn diagram.

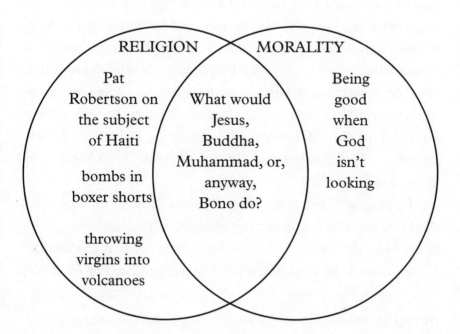

The most important part of politics in a free country, the law, falls mostly into the category of being good while God isn't looking. God is love, and the law won't even cuddle.

The fact that law can't be made identical to morality is not just a matter of the legal impracticalities in punishing all moral lapses. (You can make me *share,* but you can't make me *care.*) In a democracy the law must be exact, so we know exactly whether we're obeying it and exactly how to change it if we don't feel like obeying. Love is not as exacting as law. Even our mothers wouldn't love us if it were. But they do.

Mom's fond trait (and we'll put her in the nursing home anyway) stems from the same root as all morality—from the Old Testament love, when the Lord "saw every thing that he had made, and behold, it was very good," even the bugs. From the graciousness of the Buddha whose first precept was "Not to kill, to have regard for life, human, animal, and vegetable, not to destroy carelessly."[27] Not to ride our bikes across the lawn of our mean, crazy neighbor Mr. Norbert. From the mercy of Christ who told us to "love thy neighbor as thyself." Never mind that Mr. Norbert is chasing us with a rake. And from the opening words of the Qur'an, which have nothing to do with wiping Israel off the face of the map (something the Romans had done already in 70 AD), but say, "In the name of God, Most Gracious, Most Merciful."

Love, grace, and mercy are absolute. Law is the opposite. And not because law is hateful, clumsy, and unkind—all of the time. Human laws are the reverse of the laws of the infinite because our laws are arbitrary. They need to be. For example,

27. Per *Buddhism: Its Doctrines and Its Methods,* Alexandra David-Neel, London, 1939.

sooner or later we need to declare people to be legally dead. It would be interesting if we could see the soul depart, perhaps on gossamer wings looking a bit like the Rock in his tutu in the movie *Tooth Fairy* (or, in different garb, plunging down the sewer grate in smoke and flames). But we have only human knowledge so we must rely on things like heartbeat or brain waves or whether the dead guy's kids have finished divvying up his truck, Tampa time-share, and Ski-Doo. And when does life begin, legally? Right-to-life activists claim they know. But what if the soul is in the egg and we have to arrest every ovulating woman who failed to get laid? What if it's in the sperm, and every adolescent boy has to be tried on a hundred million counts of manslaughter? In regard to this question the U.S. Congress says, to put it in parliamentary terms, "Dunno." But law courts need to decide. Somebody—whether he's the size of a pinhead or has been in a coma since Spiro Agnew resigned—owns that truck, Tampa time-share, and Ski-Doo. It's the law.

The problem with human lawmaking is that we fail to remember we're only human (and some of our lawmakers can barely claim that). We—sometimes—make laws that are moral to the best of our knowledge, but we—always—forget that the best of our knowledge is worth squat.

Easy examples of this hubris abound. For my sins I'll take a hard one: human embryo stem cell research. People who know more about medicine than I do, which is everyone who knows anything about it, say that such research is valuable. I'll stipulate its value. People who know more about my religion than I do, such as the pope, oppose it. I'm not going to argue Catholicism with Benedict XVI. I'm given to understand that the frozen human embryos upon whom the research will be conducted are "left-overs," but as a male of sixty-three the same can be said about me. The embryos will not develop into adults capable of being doctors and popes. Neither will I. But I've had chicken pox, measles, scarlet fever, and cancer. I'm alive because of medical research, much of which seemed morally dubious when it was begun. My own deep philosophical thinking about frozen human embryo stem cell research goes no further than that the whole idea of frozen human embryos, let alone what's done to them with tweezers, creeps me out. I'm happy—this is one of the consolations of advancing age—that I don't have to make the decision.

Still I was furious when the president of the United States made the decision for me. On March 9, 2009, the president signed an executive order rescinding the previous president's executive order that banned federal funding for human embryo stem cell research. Whether such research is wrong is something I will leave to the judgment of those who have better morals than I have. My morals are sufficient, however, for determining that President Obama was damn wrong.

The White House Office of the Press Secretary released a statement titled "Remarks of President Barack Obama—As Prepared for Delivery. Signing of Stem Cell Executive Order and Scientific Integrity Presidential Memorandum." Herein was a perfect display of political immorality.

The president said, "The full promise of stem cell research remains unknown, and it should not be overstated." He then overstated it. "To regenerate a severed spinal cord and lift someone from a wheelchair. To spur insulin production and spare a child from a lifetime of needles. To treat Parkinson's, cancer, heart disease and others that afflict millions of Americans and the people who love them." (And note the politically astute touch of modern morality at the end: My dad's sick. My kid's hurting. But let's not make it all about *them*. I'm worried and hassled too.)

"Medical miracles do not happen simply by accident," the president went on to say. "They result from painstaking and costly research—from years of lonely trial and error, much of which never bears fruit—and from a government willing to support that work."

Thus it was that without King George's courtiers winding kite string for Ben Franklin and splitting firewood and flipping eye charts to advance his painstaking and costly research into lightning, stoves, and bifocals, Ben's years of lonely trial and error never did bear fruit. Today we think that the bright flash in a summer sky is God with static cling on his socks. We heat our homes by burning piles of pithy, plagiarized sayings from *Poor Richard's Almanac* in the middle of the floor. And we stare at our knitting through the bottom of old Coke bottles. We'd probably have telephones and lightbulbs by now if President Rutherford B. Hayes (a Republican) had been willing to support the work of Alexander Graham Bell and Thomas Edison. As President Obama said, "When governments fail to make these investments, opportunities are missed." (Although the lightbulbs would have to be replaced by dim, flickering fluorescent devices, anyway, to combat global climate change.)

At no point did the president acknowledge that these government "investments" are made with our money. Or that that money can be taken from us and given to people doing research on human embryos only because the government has the legal monopoly on deadly force. (Pay your taxes or get fined. Pay the fine or go to jail. Stay in jail or get shot trying to escape and join the Tea Party movement.) We have a legislative mechanism by which the monopoly is supposed to be controlled; it's called legislation. If the people of our country absolutely insist on paying the bill for frozen human embryos to be pulled apart with tweezers, Congress can pass a law. Where, exactly, in the Constitution is this moral power over our money handed off to an executive order? (No doubt the same criticism could be made of George W. Bush's executive order forbidding our money to be spent on human embryo stem cell research. But, speaking for myself, I don't get as constitutionally riled at presidents who leave my billfold alone.)

Instead of addressing any of these moral concerns, President Obama said, "Many thoughtful and decent people are conflicted about, or strongly oppose, this research." Then he called himself a liar. "The majority of Americans—from across the political spectrum, and of all backgrounds and beliefs—have come to a *consensus* that we should pursue this research." (Italics added by someone from a Republican, pro-life, Catholic background.)

But the most morally offensive thing the president said in his signing remarks was that "in recent years, when it comes to stem cell research, rather than furthering discovery, our government has forced what I believe is a false choice between sound science and moral values."

A false choice is no choice at all—Tweedledee/Tweedledum, Nancy Pelosi/Harry Reid, Joe Biden/Joe Biden. Science is, per *Webster's Third International Dictionary,* definition 1, "possession of knowledge as distinguished from ignorance or misunderstanding." Let us look at the various things science has "known" in the past three thousand years.

Thunder is the fart of Thor.

The periodic table consists of Earth, Wind, and Fire and a recording of "Got to Get You Into My Life."

The world is flat with signs near the edges saying, "Here Be Democrats."

You can turn lead into gold without a federal bailout.

We are the center of the universe and the sun revolves around us (and shines out of Uranus, Mr. President, if I may be allowed a moment of utter sophomoricism).

But, lest anyone think that this teasing of science lacks moral gravitas, let us consult—and be appalled by—the following passages from the 1910–11 eleventh edition of the *Encyclopaedia Britannica*, that great compendium of all the knowledge science possessed, carefully distinguished from ignorance and misunderstanding, as of a hundred years ago.

> . . . the negro would appear to stand on a lower evolutionary plane than the white man, and to be more closely related to the highest anthropoids.

> Mentally the negro is inferior to the white.

> . . . after puberty sexual matters take the first place in the negro's life and thought.

The above are quoted—*not* out of context—from the article titled "Negro," written by Dr. Walter Francis Willcox, professor of social science and statistics at Cornell and chief statistician of the U.S. Census Bureau. A politician!

Politicians shouldn't be allowed to make any moral decisions. They shouldn't be allowed to decide whether to shit or go
blind, a decision that might be morally painful for a politician if
he isn't polling well with the shits.

8

Taxes

Taxes are a good thing. "Every tax," said Adam Smith, "is to the person who pays it a badge, not of slavery, but of liberty. It denotes that he is subject to government, indeed, but that, as he has some property, he cannot himself be the property of a master."[28]

We're tempted to answer Smith with the "We don't need no stinking badges" quote from the movie *Treasure of the Sierra Madre,* but the sage of economic freedom has a point. We cannot be expected to surrender rights in our property—that is, pay taxes—unless we are understood to have property rights, and chief among property rights is our right to the property of ourselves. We're free. Even when taxes are levied by force, first they have to catch us.

Also, taxes caused democracy. When England's Charles I had to go, crown in hand, to beg Parliament for tax revenues, an elected body was able to claim sovereignty and dispatch with the divine right of kings (and King Charles's head).

Our own Revolutionary War was precipitated by taxes. "No taxation without representation" was a slogan among the

---

28. *The Wealth of Nations,* Book V, chapter 2.

American patriots, a crowd of whom would protest such taxes
at the Boston Tea Party in 1773. (And the original Tea Partiers,
like their later-day namesakes, were regarded with contempt by
well-placed know-it-alls. Peter Oliver, chief justice of Massachusetts, said of Samuel Adams, "He never failed of employing his
Abilities to the vilest Purposes."[29])

The French revolution, too, was a result of taxes. Louis XVI
needed to raise them and, looking to do so, convened the states-
general, a group of delegates from the nobility, the clergy, and
the commoners. A cutthroat bunch they proved to be.

We owe a lot to our taxes. But we owe a lot *on* our taxes too.
That is why the most surprisingly good thing about taxes is that
they are a good deal.

The American government will spend $4 trillion this year.
There are an estimated 308.6 million Americans. We each get
$12,956. Sure we mostly get it in the form of Sacramento light
rail projects that don't go anywhere except Sacramento, sugar
beet price supports, contributions to the charity known as GM,
Afghanistan troop surges, and interest payments on Chinese-
owned T bills. We'd rather have cash. But, still, $12,956 isn't
bad.

Let's say you're a family of five: a dad, a mom, and three
lovely kids. You're the kind of family we conservatives endorse.
You're getting $64,781 from the government. Even Republicans
are on the dole. Dad (conservative women are proud to be stay-
at-home moms) will have to make a pile of money to pay $65K
in taxes.

---

29. *Peter Oliver's Origin and Progress of the American Rebellion: A Tory's
View*, ed. Douglass Adair and John A. Schutz, Stanford University
Press, 1961.

Although it is unclear just how big a pile dad will have to make to ensure that he's feeding, sheltering, and grooming the America of the future rather than sucking her teat.

Democrats in Congress may lower taxes, for fear that more Republicans will be elected. Or Democrats in Congress may raise taxes for fear more Republicans will be elected before Democrats have a chance to enact a tax hike. The president may make all Wall Street profits greater than the 2009 Madoff-investor average return subject to punitive capitation. Or the president may give another squillion-jillion dollars in bailout funds to all Wall Street firms. The tax code is so confusing that every time a federal appointment is made the appointee has to go before a congressional committee to explain how he got so confused that he didn't pay his taxes. And taxes—and loans to government that will have to be repaid with taxes—come in a variety of types and kinds. Personal income tax receipts fund less than a quarter of federal outlays. Corporate taxes provide a whopping 3.8 percent. Borrowed money accounts for nearly half of what Washington will spend this year. The deficit gap will be closed by revenue from that $9 pack of cigarettes you just bought because thinking about taxes stresses you out.

Natasha Altamirano of the National Taxpayers Union did some complicated mathematics and said, "By my reckoning, somewhere between 85 and 95 million households out of 115 million total have a smaller tax liability than the per capita spending burden." This means that the breadwinners for between one-fifth and one-quarter of American households are shoveling coal in the engine rooms of the ship of state while everybody else is a stowaway, necking with Kate Winslet like Leonardo DiCaprio in *Titanic*.

Ms. Altamirano went on to note that those breadwinners doing all the work are also less likely to be receiving any kind of government monetary assistance and are more likely to have their Social Security benefits taxed.

"If we were to compensate for this," she said, "I imagine that more like 100 million households have a smaller liability than the per capita spending burden." One hundred out of 115 is 87 percent. Our nation is 87 percent mooch, 87 percent leach, 87 percent "Spare (hope and) change, man?"

It may be worse than that or, depending on how greedily liberal you are, better. Let's abandon the complicated mathematics of taxation. We don't understand complicated mathematics. We were liberal arts majors. If we understood complicated mathematics we'd be wealthy hedge fund managers in prison. Let's go to arithmetic. The U.S. gross domestic product for 2009 has been calculated by the Department of Commerce's Bureau of Economic Analysis as $14.2 trillion. The Federal Budget, being $4 trillion is (divide 4 by 14.2, move the decimal point two places to the right, add the thingy over the numeral 5 on your keyboard) 28.2 percent of the gross domestic product. Let's round down and call it one-fourth. This is our real rate of national taxation. The government makes off with one-fourth of our goods and services. Then the government gives those goods and services back to us. (In a slightly altered form, the way a horse gives the hay we feed it back to us in a slightly altered form.) We each get our $12,956, which is our per-person share of one-fourth of the gross domestic product. But, since the real tax rate on that GDP is 25 percent, each of us has to make $51,824 a year—our per person share of the GDP—to be entitled to call ourselves a tax*payer,* not a tax vampire. And we have to make $259,120 a year if we're supporting a family of five.

Slightly confused by this? Democrats always have been.

How many American households make a quarter of a million bucks? The president's does, and with only two kids. The president is taxing himself. Good. But the rest of the U.S. government's operating expenses are being funded by paycheck withholding on Conan O'Brien's NBC settlement. Plus there's all the money the government has borrowed by taking out a second mortgage on North America, which will soon have the Treasury Department calling the toll-free number for the "debt restructuring services" advertised on late night TV.

The gross unfairness of America's tax system won't lead to class war. Or, if it does, the war will be brief. There are 300 million of us SpongeBobs and hardly any of the sucker fish we're soaking. On the other hand, young people—with no dependents except their Twitter pals—have to earn only double their age to be ladling gravy to Uncle Sam. They could turn on the government if they started thinking about this (or anything).

The rest of us? We're in the clover. True, we have to "give" 25 percent of our workweek to the IRS. That's ten hours—all of Wednesday and half of Thursday morning. But it's still a good deal and doesn't really leave us overburdened on the job. Nothing gets done on Monday and Friday anyway. Tuesday we had to go pick up our kid from school because a peanut was discovered in the food dish belonging to the fifth grade's gerbil and the whole building had to be hypoallergized. On Thursday, after an early lunch, we left a full cup of coffee in our cubicle and draped our suit jacket over the back of our chair, so it would look like we were around the office someplace, and caught a Nationals game. We don't have to worry that out-of-control federal spending or an insane tax structure will wreck our lives. We've got government jobs.

9

More Taxes

I take it back. Taxes aren't a good thing. This is because (as I mentioned before but forgot this time) you're very rich. You're surprised to learn that you're very rich, especially when, like me, you're really broke. But, if you think about it, you know you're rich because only a rich person can afford to pay double for everything.

And you do. The financial bailout, for example. You paid for it once when you discovered that your retirement savings consisted of nothing but half a chocolate bunny from last Easter, three paper clips, and a dried-up Sharpie. Then you paid for it again with your tax dollars and with the permanent damage done to the American economy when the government pawned everything in the nation because your tax dollars weren't enough to pay for the bailout.

Likewise with the economic stimulus. You write checks to cover your mortgage payment, utilities, insurance premiums, car loan, basic cable, Visa, MasterCard, and American Express bills, and you hand fistfuls of cash to your children and turn them loose in the Abercrombie & Fitch store. Think you're done stimulating the economy? Think again. The president of the United States is also on an economically stimulating spending spree, and he's paying for it with a lien on all the future job and business opportunities that your children will have. This means they won't have them. I hope that your kids, once they've gotten their MBAs, enjoy stocking shelves at the Dollar Store.

What about the new car you paid for with taxpayer funds given to GM and Chrysler? How come it isn't in the driveway? You gave all that money to the car companies and they didn't even send a thank-you note on a scratch-and-sniff card with that new car smell. No, if you want a new car you have to—you guessed it—pay double.

Of course maybe you got something out of the Cash for Clunkers program. And good for you if you did. At least, when you bought a new car, you didn't pay GM or Chrysler twice; you paid Nissan once. (Meanwhile, will some liberal brainbox explain to me why it's a good thing to junk a useful machine? How does destroying something that's worth money make us worth more money?)

Paying double for everything didn't start with the financial crisis or even with Democratic control of Congress. Paying double is an integral part of the modern welfare state.

Beginning with welfare. Your tax dollars pay for federal, state, and local welfare programs. Then you pay for your daughter to pursue a career in "holistic dance liberation." You subsidize your son's Internet start-up idea—Buttbook, a Web site you go on with all your enemies. Plus there's your perennial bum of a brother-in-law, tweaking on meth in the doublewide and watching Cartoon Network on the high-definition television you paid for.

Same with schools. Your school taxes pay for Alger Hiss Public High School, conveniently right down the street, inconveniently full of heroin and 9mm handguns. So you also pay tuition at Friar Torquemata Parochial High.

At school, home, or work the most important function of government is to protect your person and property. That's what the police department is for. And you get to pay the police *and* pay for burglar alarms, private security patrols, and guard dogs, such as our family's guard dog, Pinky-Wink. (For the information of any prospective burglars, Pinky-Wink isn't really a Boston terrier. He's . . . um . . . a Rhodesian ridgeback, weighing 100 . . . make that 150 pounds. Uh, the kids named him. Stop yapping, Pinky-Wink.)

The second most important function of government, in my opinion, is trash pickup. And people in government can start with themselves, as far as I'm concerned. Anyway, municipal garbage collectors pick up the trash from your house. But not until you've sorted it into the proper recycling bins, which you do by picking up the trash from your house. With government, what you don't pay double for in money you pay double for in time and effort.

But usually it's money. When you pay a hospital bill you're really paying two hospital bills—one bill for you because you have a job and/or private insurance and can pay the hospital and another bill, which is tacked onto your bill, to cover the medical expenses of someone who doesn't have a job and/or private insurance and can't pay the hospital. Your tennis elbow underwrites the Alger Hiss Public High School student's 9mm handgun wound.

And never is paying double as doubly troubling as it is in the matter of retirement. You have to pay into Social Security

and into your IRA and your Keogh plan and put some money
in your savings account too. You have to pay Medicare tax and
buy Medicare supplemental insurance and contribute to a medical savings account and make doctor bill copayments besides.
And the funding for Social Security and Medicare is so under-
financed and actuarially shaky that you cannot be certain those
programs will exist by the time you're eligible for them. And
you're 64½.

Would you like to know what taxpayers are getting out of
this deal? You and me both. How do we benefit from this twin-
ning, this twoing, this duality? Damned if I can figure it out.
Barkeep, make that a double.

10

Being Penny-Wise

One thing that can be said in favor of our political system is that it doesn't change much or often, for better or for worse. The American government is a body of enormous mass, subject to considerable friction, but possessing tremendous momentum. This explains why we learned nothing in that high school civics class. If we wanted to understand government we should have paid more attention to the high school physics class we flunked.

Or gotten a job on the railroad. Government is a mile of boxcars filled with lard. The locomotive is, at best, the Little Engine That Could and more often something from Lionel. You and I are unlikely to get this train moving by pushing on the caboose even if we get all our friends to help. But once it's in motion we'd better not stand in its way. Derailment is an option if we pry up the tracks. What a mess. And this metaphor is making less sense than a physics lesson, especially if we take it into the switch yard of government planning.

I'll try one more time. Government isn't the vehicle for lard, government is the lardass itself, waddling slowly down the path of least resistance, changing course only when it has to because of social forest fire, public opinion mud slide, or the earthquake of war. No matter how much we wanted the government to change course, and no matter how much we approve of the new direction government has taken, we were better off without the catastrophe that made the government turn left or right.

You may like the New Deal, but a worldwide depression with its various side effects such as Hitler was a high price to pay for WPA murals. I may like Ronald Reagan, but the earth would be a happier planet if he hadn't been necessary. We applaud the outcome of the Civil War and the civil rights movement, but an alternative—less costly in blood and treasure—was to not treat black people like shit for five hundred years.

That our government can't be easily budged or deflected is beneficial to some extent. Better this than the third world plan where government is changed more often than socks. But the monumental gravity of government causes bad programs and policies not only to endure but to become enshrined. And the immovable object/irresistible force conundrum of government makes it something—a high school physics quiz, a train wreck, a vastly overweight friend who begs to come on our kayak trip— that we want to avoid.

The least little manifestation of government will suffice as an example. How much would you think it would cost the U.S. mint to produce a penny? You're half right. To manufacture this little item of pocket clutter is about twice as expensive as its nominal value. And its nominal value is nominal indeed. A penny will not buy a penny postcard or a pennywhistle or a piece of penny candy. It will not even, if you're managing the U.S. mint, buy a penny.

The problem is the cost of zinc, which is what a "copper" is actually made of. For the past twenty-five years a pennyweight of copper has been worth considerably more than a penny. And we wouldn't want our money to have any actual monetary value, would we? That would violate all of the economic thinking that has been done since John Maynard Keynes. Therefore the United States began making pennies out of less expensive zinc with a thin plating of copper for the sake of tradition and to keep Lincoln from looking like he'd been stamped out of a galvanized feed trough. But then a rising commodities market drove up zinc prices. (Maybe China needs a lot of zinc for, oh, I don't know, stabilizing the lead paint on Barbie dolls so that our girls don't start beating their girls on math tests, or something.)

I learned about the penny's cost overrun in one of those little five- or six-column-inch filler items that are now the mainstay of the once-mighty wire services. This particular squib ran a while ago in the *Boston Globe,* but I didn't come across it until recently. I buy the *Globe* only for the comics, the Sudoku, and to train the puppy. I was arranging the sheets of newsprint on the kitchen floor, being careful to keep the editorial pages facedown. (I don't want to give any encouragement to the Boston terrier's natural inbred liberalism.) Anyway, there was the penny article.

I suppose, as a fiscal conservative and—at least until the cocktail hour—a responsible citizen, I should have been indignant. But, to tell the truth, I was hopping about with glee. (Something that, by the way, is not advisable in a kitchen's puppy-training area.) You see, there are times when even we staunchest of libertarians lose our faith, or our faithlessness. That is to say, we lose our faith in our loss of faith in government. We catch ourselves thinking things like, "Whoa, what about the subprime mortgage market? That *sub* part was one moldy hoagie. Maybe there *should* be more government regulatory oversight." Or, "Wait a minute, just because I've been to the emergency room for string trimmer injuries six times in the past two years is no reason for my health insurance to be canceled. Since when is stupidity a preexisting condition?"

Libertarians are only human. When we're tired and stressed we're occasionally vulnerable to the kind of easy self-gratification and delusional thinking that leads to government dependency. But then comes a story like the penny costing two pennies and it's instant cold turkey.

In for a penny, in for $16 million of wasted tax dollars spent to put eight billion pennies into circulation each year. Take care of the pennies and the pounds (of flesh extracted by the IRS) will take care of themselves. A penny for your thoughts, and I'm not just picking your brain; I'm offering a 100 percent return on investment.

The good news is you have a lot more money than you thought you did. We all do. A quick survey of my home indicates that the average American household has something on the order of a million pennies stashed in coffee cans, cigar boxes, quart jars, kitchen junk drawers, children's piggy banks, under car seats, between couch cushions, plus the two pennies in my old loafers from junior high in a box in the attic. So it's new home theater–sized flat screen TVs all 'round as soon as we get done building our backyard zinc smelters.

The bad news is that government is not just inert but corruptly inert. Various public interest groups with (excuse me) "common cents" have been trying to get rid of the penny for years. The Treasury Department itself does not like wasting $16 million a year on pennies when there are still so many banks, investment firms, and insurance companies in need of huge executive bonuses. The penny is a coin slot-jamming curse to the vending machine industry. It is a cash register pantload and change-making pain to retailers (not to mention a barrier to rounding all prices up a nickel). And the artificial demand for zinc created by the penny is anathema to the companies that have to pay more for zinc as a result. Everyone from the makers of buckets to the purveyors of cream to spread on cute lifeguard noses is mad at the penny.

But to no avail. According to the somewhat smelly and discolored *Boston Globe,* Jarden Zinc Products, the nation's only supplier of the zinc "blanks" from which pennies are struck, has managed to block legislation banishing the penny. It has done so mainly by paying the political consulting firm Baker & Daniels LLP $180,000 to lobby against such legislation.

Then again, is this really bad news? It's not great that we the public are paying double for something that isn't worth a red cent. But it is rather wonderful that for a mere $180,000 you can get government to sit there like a lump. Consider how many times in history governments should have sat there like a lump. What if Japan's bombing of Pearl Harbor, Austria-Hungary's commencement of the First World War, or Napoleonic France's invasion of Russia could have been prevented for $180,000. Ah, the miracle of democracy—always letting us get our 2¢ in.

PART II

What Is to Be Done?

Sometimes it is said that man cannot be trusted with the government of himself. Can he then be trusted with the government of others?
                    —Thomas Jefferson, First Inaugural Address

The U.S.S. Thresher Bailout and the Washing-Machine-for-Her-Birthday Stimulus Plan

Did the 2008–2009 bailout of banks and financial institutions work? Well, here we are, a bit recessed but not suffering from a Great Depression. If John Steinbeck were alive and writing his Pulitzer Prize–winning proletarian novel, the Joads would be fleeing the rust belt rather than the dust bowl, and they'd still be headed toward a chimerical paradise of economic plenty, though, in this case, Washington. Instead of a Flivver, they'd be packed into a Nissan Murano, down payment courtesy of Cash for Clunkers. And the grapes in *The Grapes of Wrath* would be zinfandel.

As for the stimulus plan, the results seem to be PG-13 at best. Opinions differ on how stimulated we are. Whatever Harry Reid is feeling, Miranda Cosgrove on podcast does nothing for me.

Here, according to the Congressional Budget Office, are some of the spending programs authorized by the $787 billion "American Recovery and Reinvestment Act of 2009."

$9.3 billion to "Invest in rail transportation" (Last train to Clarksville!)

$6 billion to "Clean up sites formerly used by the Defense Department" (Find someplace to bury "Don't Ask, Don't Tell.")

$4.6 billion to "Provide additional money to the Army Corps of Engineers" (A basement dehumidifier for the French Quarter.)

$4 billion to "Provide additional financing for state and local law enforcement" (Taser guns for school crossing guards.)

$4 billion to "Repair and modernize public housing units" (Where would you like this crate of bioengineered cockroaches, Mrs. Gilhooey?")

$3.2 billion to "Provide tax break to General Motors" (We broke Oldsmobile, we broke Pontiac . . .)

$2.8 billion to "Provide additional money to the Department of Homeland Security" ("Secretary Napolitano, we just received this fax from Nigeria, from highly placed Umar Farouk Abdulmutallab. We could make a fortune!")

$2.5 billion to "Provide additional financing to improve communications in rural areas" ("I'm away down here in the holler, Clem! Ain't heard a word yer sayin'! Why doncha use that there new megaphone you got from the government man?")

$2 billion to "Provide additional child care" (Give an extra sawbuck to the babysitter and let her buy her own six-pack.)

$2 billion to "Support battery manufacture" (Every toy imported from China will be required by law to be "batteries not included.")

$2 billion to "Finance renovations and technology upgrade at community health centers" (New rectal thermometers for all.)

$1.3 billion to "Invest in air transportation" (The bad news: they're charging you $50 for each piece of carry-on baggage. The good news: you get to lie down in the overhead bin.)

$1.2 billion to "Construct and repair veterans' hospitals and cemeteries" ("Found a place to bury 'Don't Ask, Don't Tell'!")

$1 billion to "Provide water to rural areas and Western areas impacted by draught" ("Here's a bottle of Pellegrino for you, and a bottle of Pellegrino for *you*, and . . .)

$1 billion to "Provide money for 2010 census" ("Counted eleventy more Martha Coakley voters hiding in the Big Dig!")

$830 million to "Provide additional financing for the National Oceanic and Atmospheric Administration" (Sun's out! Surf's up!)

$650 million to "Provide coupon to convert to digital television" ("Hey, Lulu May, come on up outa the holler! *Hee-Haw* reruns is on TVLand!")

$555 million to "Help defense employees sell homes" (Paint walls a neutral color. Keep lawn trimmed. Flowers in a jar on the kitchen counter add a homey touch for prospective buyers.)

$510 million to "Repair and modernize 4,200 Native American housing units" (Hold on 17, double down on face cards and tens.)

$500 million to "Help states and local school districts track student data and improve teacher quality" (Everybody's grades have been posted on Facebook. Bow and muzzle-loader season on teachers opens November 1.)

$500 million to "Help states find jobs for unemployed workers" (Get your brother-in-law a job making lists of strange things the federal government is spending stimulus money on in your state.)

$400 million to "Provide grants to states for energy-efficient vehicles and infrastructure" (Mr. Mayor, here's your bike.)

$300 million to "Provide incentives for hiring disadvantaged workers" (Unless their disadvantage is that they're here illegally from Guatemala and are willing to work doing anything.)

$300 million to "Replace older vehicles owned by the federal government with hybrid and electric cars" ("Mr. President, it's Segway 1.")

$231 million to "Expand national service program" ("My name is Ben Bernanke, I'll be your server tonight. The specials are incredibly expensive . . .")

$192 million to "Equalize mass transit and parking benefits" (New York City will park its subway cars in your carport, but you can park your SUV on the subway tracks.)

$70 million to "Help states provide services to homeless children" ("Kids, if you'd care to be seated on this piece of cardboard on the sidewalk, Ben will take your drink orders.")

And so on with ninety-four other interesting ways to spend your tax dollars.

Assuming the American economy needed a stimulus, there was an alternate way to provide it. For only a couple of hundred billion more than the cost of the Recovery and Reinvestment Act (and who's even counting anymore?), all federal personal income taxes could have been eliminated for a year. (Personal income tax receipts were estimated at $953 billion in 2009.[30])

---

30. Note ugly drop in personal income tax receipts since 2008.

This was the suggestion of my ex-congressman in the Second District of New Hampshire, Charlie Bass. With his display of common sense, you can see why Charlie is my *ex*-congressman.

A yearlong tax holiday would be quite the stimulus around my house. Muffin, age twelve, could get a webcam to put on her own *iCarly*-type show except with more giggling. Poppet, age ten, has been begging for a herd of miniature Nubian goats and a chance for a slot on the national goat rodeo circuit. We would be able to pay for her fancy, spangled goat-roping outfits, no problem. Buster, age six, wants a child-sized *Enola Gay* with nerf A-bomb. My wife would like to drive her Kia Rondo over a cliff. And I have my eye on a new muzzle-loader so I can bag Mr. Mannsburden, my high school civics teacher, if he's still alive.

The advantage of a tax abatement over a stimulus plan is that, instead of idiots in Washington spending your and my money, us idiots get to spend our own. Our spending will be foolish, but not as foolish as government spending for the simple reason of Committee Brain—individuals aren't as stupid as a group. It's the difference between Harvard and the Harvard football team, which any eleven kids from the Pop Warner League back where I come from in Ohio could whip by a dozen TDs without resort to the forward pass.

Speaking of stupid people from Harvard—and that would be you Larry Summers—how about the federal bailout? We'll take it as a given that the bailout was effective. That is, a bankruptcy judge wasn't sitting on the ATM when I went to use it at lunch hour. But it's hard to imagine that we taxpayers pulled all those singed, stinking bank and financial institution chestnuts out of the fire without causing a moral hazard.

"Moral hazard" is the term economists use for a situation that reduces the incentive to avoid bad economic behavior. If you have an insurance policy for $1 million on a house that's worth $150,000, and you're behind on your mortgage payments anyway, you'll be less careful when lighting your gas grill. In fact you may drag your gas grill into the middle of the living room and light it there, adding some gasoline in case it doesn't catch.

The message that the U.S. government sent to the broke banks and beggared financial institutions was: "Don't you ever do this again or we'll give you more money." After which there was a flurry of government regulatory activity to make sure it was illegal to do "this" again. And the banks and financial institutions won't do "this" again. They'll do "that."

John H. Cochrane, professor of finance at the University of Chicago, wrote a thoroughgoing article, "Lessons from the Financial Crisis," in the winter 2009–10 issue of the Cato Institute's *Regulation* magazine. Professor Cochrane pointed out that "the regulatory system ends up encouraging artificial obscurity." Make the rules tougher and they'll play the game tougher. Are the people named Masters of Regulation likely to be quicker and better motivated than the people named Masters of the Universe?

Besides, as Professor Cochrane noted, "It was the regulated, supervised part of the market that failed." I've known Chris Cox for more than twenty years. Chris was head of the Securities and Exchange Commission when the financial crisis began. He was a congressman before his appointment. The average IQ in the House of Representatives dropped fifty points when he left, and what little moral capital there was in Congress sank to almost nothing. Still the bastards outwitted him. There are ten million people in the world trying to be the Salomon Brothers and nobody's trying to be Chris Cox.

Financial regulations are law, but finance is mathematics, and Chris Cox is brilliant, but he's a brilliant lawyer. What tipped the whistle-blowers on the Bernie Madoff scheme was not whether all of Madoff's regulatory filings had been duly signed and witnessed but the fact that Madoff's return on investment was too steady. Not too high, too steady. The thing that troubled people who are mathematically inclined—notably Boston investment analyst Harry Markopolos—was how no formula of investment, no algorithm of trades, could be created to reproduce Madoff's returns. With the benefit of hindsight, you could make trades that were more profitable than Madoff's. And lots of people made trades that were less profitable than Madoff's. But nobody could flatline the high yields like Bernie. The trustees of Brandeis University didn't see the problem. The rest of us wouldn't have known what the rub was if it was down our shorts.

As for the works of our current regulators, Professor Cochrane said, "A lot of policy seems aimed at stopping anyone from ever again losing money in financial dealings." Try that at the Indian casino blackjack table. If you voted for Obama often enough, it might work. Said the good professor, "To give government officials the power to bail out firms at their discretion, especially if those officials are elected or political appointees, is practically to guarantee a bailout."

Kill the spending. Fuck the regulations. Marry an investment banker.

2

And While We're at It . . .

Hello? Bailout people? Mr. Secretary of the Treasury? Aren't you forgetting somebody? Like me? I'm a print journalist. Talk about financial crisis! Print journalists may soon have to send their kids to public schools, feed dry food to their cats, and give up their leases on Honda Insights and get the Hummers that are being offered at such deep discounts these days.

The print journalism industry is taking a beating, circling the drain, running on fumes. Especially running on fumes. You could smell Frank Rich all the way to Wasilla when Sarah Palin was nominated. Not that print journalism actually emits much in the way of greenhouse gases. We have an itty-bitty carbon footprint. We're earth friendly. The current press run of an average U.S. big city daily newspaper can be made from one tree. Compare that to the global warming hot air produced by talk radio, cable TV, and Arianna Huffington.

There are many compelling reasons to save America's print journalism. And I'll think of some while the bartender brings me another drink. In the first place one out of three American households is dependent on print journalism.[31] And if you think

---

31. For puppy training.

home foreclosures are disruptive to American society, imagine what would happen if *USA Today* stopped publishing. Lose your home and you become homeless, a member of an important interest group with many respected advocates and a powerful political lobbying arm. But lose your newspaper and what are you going to do for covers on a cold night while you're sleeping on a park bench? Try blanketing yourself with Matt Drudge to keep warm.

The government is bailing out Wall Street for being evil and the car companies for being stupid. But print journalism brings you Paul Krugman *and* Anna Quindlen. Also, in 1898 Joseph Pulitzer of the *New York World* and William Randolph Hearst of the *New York Morning Journal* started the Spanish-American War. All the Lehman Brothers put together couldn't cause as much evil stupidity as that.

Moreover, rescuing print journalism is a two-fer. Not only will America's principal source of Sudoku and *Doonesbury* be preserved but so will an endangered species—the hard-bitten, cynical, heavy-drinking newshound with a press card in his hatband, a cigarette stub dangling from his lip, and free ring-side prizefight tickets tucked into his vest pocket. These guys don't reproduce in captivity. And there are hardly any of them left in the wild. I checked the bar. Just Mike Barnicle, as usual. How's tricks, Mike? Where'd everybody go? Sun's over the yardarm. Time to pour lunch.

We print journalists are victims of economic forces beyond our control. We were as surprised as everyone else was by the sudden collapse of the reliable reporting market. We had no idea that real news and clear-eyed analysis were being "bundled" with subprime celebrity gossip, *U.S. Weekly* derivatives, and Jennifer Aniston/Sarah Jessica Parker swaps. We need a swift infusion of federal aid. Otherwise all the information in America will be about Lindsay Lohan's sex life.

Saving print journalism will be a bargain for the U.S. government. Nothing approaching $787 billion is required in our case. We'll settle for having the Treasury Department pay our tab at the Washington Palm. True, there is the danger that network television, with its much higher potential losses, will demand equal treatment. But this cannot be justified. Network television has been attempting to lure viewers for years with its low-interest-programming only to have those viewers discover that their brains are bankrupt.

Some taxpayers may object to a print journalism bailout on the grounds that it mostly benefits the liberal elite. And we can't blame taxpayers for being reluctant to subsidize the reportorial careers of J-school twerps who should have joined the Peace Corps and gone to Africa to "speak truth to power" to Robert Mugabe. Senators and congressmen may have their objections as well. They want first call on those twerps themselves. Twerps make excellent Hill staffers and can help elected officials angle for appointment to high positions in the administration, such as Boxer Shorts Bomb Czar. Obviously more twerps will be available if print journalism doesn't exist anymore. But I think we can ask America's legislators to make this sacrifice. (Memo to pols from an old press hack, strictly on the q.t.: the J-school twerps don't smoke, don't drink, do yoga, and will tell dailykos.com if you paw them.) And I think we can ask taxpayers whether they would prefer to pay journalists to harmlessly tickle keyboards at the *New Republic* or whether they would prefer to pay journalists to be in positions of influence on political policies that will wreck the taxpayers' lives.

Remember, America, you can't wrap a fish in satellite radio or line the bottom of your birdcage with MSNBC (however appropriate that would be). It's expensive to swat flies with a BlackBerry. Newsboys tossing flat screen monitors onto your porch will damage the wicker furniture. And a dog that's trained to piddle on your wireless router can cause a dangerous electrical short circuit and burn down your house.

3

Generation Vex

The financial crisis did not begin in September 2008; it began on October 15, 2007, and was reported the next day by the Associated Press.

> The nation's first baby boomer applied for Social Security Monday, the start of an avalanche of applications from the post–World War II generation.
>
> Kathleen Casey-Kirschling, a former teacher from New Jersey, applied for benefits over the Internet.
>
> Casey-Kirschling was born one second after midnight on Jan. 1, 1946, making her the first baby boomer—a generation of nearly 80 million born from 1946 to 1964.

Oh rend thy garments, America. Heap ashes upon thy head. We the generation of generations—triumphant in our multitudes, invincible, indomitable, insufferable—have come into our inheritance. Hereby we claim our birthright. Give us all your money.

The pittance that is a current Social Security payment was intended to maintain the decrepit retirees of yore in their accustomed condition of thin gruel and single-car garages. Such

chump change will hardly suffice for today's vigorous sexage-
narians intent on (among other things) vigorous sex in places
like Paris, St. Barts, and Phuket. How can current Social Security allotments be expected to fund our skydiving, bungee
jumping, hang gliding, and whitewater rafting, our skiing, golf,
and scuba excursions, our photo safaris to Africa, bike tours
of Tuscany, and sojourns at Indian ashrams, our tennis clinics,
spa treatments, gym memberships, personal fitness training,
and cosmetic surgery, our luxury cruises to the Galápagos and
Antarctica, the vacation homes in Hilton Head and Vail, the lap
pools, Jacuzzis, and clay courts being built thereat and the his
and hers Harley-Davidsons?

And we haven't even touched on the subject of Social Security's civil union life partner, Medicare. It won't take much skydiving, bungee jumping, hang gliding, and whitewater rafting
before we all require new hips, knees, and elbows, fused spinal
discs, pacemakers, and steel plates in our heads. The expense of
these will be as nothing compared to the cost of our pharma-
cological needs. Remember, we are the generation that *knows*
drugs. We know drugs and we like drugs. From about 1967 until
John Belushi died we created a way of life based almost entirely
on drugs. And we can do it again. Except, this time, instead of
us trying to figure out how to pay for it all by selling each other
nickel bags of pot, you the taxpayer will be footing the bill. And
did I mention that we'll expect to be airlifted to the Mayo Clinic
every time we have an ache or pain? Nothing smaller than a
Gulfstream G-3, please.

So just give us all the money in the federal, state, and local
budgets. Forget spending on the military, education, or infrastructure. What with Afghanistan, falling SAT scores, and the
California freeway system buried in mud slides, it's not as if the

military, education, and infrastructure are doing very well anyway. Besides, you don't have a choice. We are 80 million strong.
That's a number equal to almost two-thirds of the registered
voters in the United States. Do what we say or we will ballot you
into a condition that will make Haiti look like Ibiza (where we'll
be staying).

And that's the good news. Emptying government coffers is
the least of the damage that we baby boomers intend to inflict
over the next thirty or forty years. What we're really up to is
something more diabolical. Our generation is going to do what
our generation has always done best. We're going to shape the
American social fabric to our will and make the entire nation
conform to our ideals, judgments, and tastes. It will be like the
Clinton administration but much, much worse. (An interesting
irony since in '08 you narrowly avoided getting a Clinton administration that was much, much worse.)

What we're going to do is make all of you old like we are—
old and dumpy and querulous and fuddled. We're achieving
it already. Look at the hip young men walking around in their
high-water pants, wearing stupid bowling shirts buttoned up to
the collar. A bunch of twenty-six-year-olds are going to coffee
shops (coffee shops! how *antique*!) dressed as their grandpas.
And what about teenage droopy drawers? That's gramp's other
fashion-forward look, perfect for a weekend of crabgrass killing
and mulching the hydrangeas.

Those great big cushy, ugly sneakers—be they ever so expensive or young athlete–endorsed—are nothing but the dread
"comfortable shoes" that have been worn forever by the geri-
atric. We have made mere schoolchildren as dependent upon

Ritalin as we are upon Lipitor and Cialis. And notice that traffic jams are everywhere, but it's not because of too many cars or too few highway lanes. It's just slow driving in the famous old-age mode, with cell phones and onboard navigation systems to provide someone with whom to have a confusing, grumpy argument even when you're alone.

What else do oldsters do besides drive slowly? They watch TV. Leave it to the baby boom to invent something that makes viewing a small screen even worse than TV—the Internet, TV that talks back! Not that we haven't done a pretty good job of worsening TV as well. Flip through the cable channels and compare what you see to what was seen a generation ago: *Jersey Shore* vs. *The Dinah Shore Show*, *The Bachelor* vs. *The Honeymooners*, *The Tonight Show* vs. *The Tonight Show*. When it comes to befuddled, is not the whole entertainment industry drooling in its second childhood?

We baby boomers are growing old, but growing old with a vengeance. Our hands may be palsied and arthritic but we hold America's fate in them. And America's fate can be summed up in one word: *youthanasia*.

4

Health Care Reform

America's politicians are making enough noise about health care costs to wake the dead (an item on the Obama second term legislative agenda). Medical care in America *is* expensive. Our country spent $2.5 trillion on health care in 2009, 17.6 percent of the gross national product—an amount equal to $8,170 per person.

We persons, on the other hand, aren't spending anywhere near that much of our take-home pay on health care. According to the U.S. Bureau of Labor Statistics, *Consumer Spending in 2007* (the most recent figures available), the average annual household out-of-pocket expenditure on health care was $2,853. This is a third of what we spent on "transportation" and 10 percent less than what we spent on the "transportation" subcategory of "vehicle purchases." (Go for a drive or stay alive?) What we spent on health care was just $185 more than what we spent on "food away from home," which, given our obesity statistics, we shouldn't be eating. If we cut down on "entertainment" ($2,698) and did something more worthwhile ("reading": $118) we'll have plenty to spend on the higher taxes that are on their way to fund less expensive health care.

★ ★ ★

What part of the cost of medical treatment is supposed to get reformed? *The* cost or *our* cost? Somehow, in the mouths of politicians, it's always both. The quality of health care will increase, the quantity of health care will increase, the number of people receiving health care will grow, and therefore health care will cost less.

It was not my proudest moment as a Republican when, in a September 2009 joint session of Congress, representative Joe Wilson of South Carolina shouted, "You lie!" at the president of the United States during the president's speech about health care reform. Joe was definitely rude, Joe was probably in violation of parliamentary rules of order, and there's the possibility that Joe was not completely sober. But was Joe wrong?

Something doesn't add up. Politicians are telling me that I can smoke, drink, gain two hundred pounds, then win an iron man triathlon at age ninety-five.

And will the reformers please quit talking about "health care providers"? What the hell is a "health care provider"? That could be some guy just off the boat from China with a fistful of rusty acupuncture needles. A "health care provider" was the school nurse when I was in third grade who gave you peppermint oil if you broke your neck on the playground. I caught Buster, my six-year-old, playing "health care provider" with one of the little girls in his first-grade class. They were filling out toy forms fully clothed.

Why does medical treatment in America cost so much? It's not because doctors are getting richer. In 2009 the *Archives of*

Internal Medicine published a study showing that between 1995 and 2003 the average annual income of primary care physicians dropped by 10.2 percent to $146,405, a lot less than we pay Joe Biden.

One problem leading to high health care costs is the liability lawyer, of course, with his face up on billboards everywhere: "You Might Have Been Maltreated On by a Doctor and Not Even Know It." But I don't want to make anyone ill by bringing up the subject of John Edwards.

A worse problem is that we're getting what we pay for. Sally Pipes (no relation to the previously cited Richard Pipes) is the president of the Pacific Research Institute think tank in San Francisco. She is the author of two books and numerous articles about health care and has been named by *Forbes* as one of the world's thirty leading experts on the subject. In *The Top Ten Myths of American Health Care*[32] Pipes notes that for a man born in the United States in 1900 there was an almost one in five chance of dying before his first birthday. Now a man has to live to be my age before the annual mortality rate is one in five, which is why I'm careful with things like stairs and go down to the wine cellar only four times on any given evening.

We are, Pipes says, paying fourteen times as much for medical treatment as we were in 1950, but since then our life expectancy has increased by ten years. It's not a spectacular bargain. Life expectancy in 1950 was sixty-eight and, by my calculation, for fourteen times as much money we should be living to age 952. But Medicare is already overburdened. And imagine getting trapped on a Carnival cruise with some old fart who can't stop complaining about how nobody cooks pig bladder the way

---

32. Pacific Research Institute, 2008.

they did in 1066. Ten years isn't bad. I may live to see a Massachusetts Republican elected to the Senate.

All that money hasn't done much to cure Alzheimer's. On
the other hand, says Pipes, between 1950 and 2000 the death
rate for heart disease, America's number one cause of mortality (not counting forgetting your wedding anniversary, which I
blame on Alzheimer's), was reduced by 59 percent. And America's rate of infant mortality has gone from twenty-nine per one
thousand live births in 1950 to fewer than seven.

Yes, yes, but other countries have done better while spending less, say health care reformers. There are almost thirty other
countries where life expectancy is longer than it is in the United
States.

Other countries are not the United States, Pipes points out.
America's homicide rate was 5.9 per 100,000 people in 2004.
Canada's was 1.95. Germany's was .98. America had 14.25 traffic fatalities per 100,000 people in 2006. Canada had 9.25. And
France had 7.4 because the French sit around in cafés all day
and don't go anywhere except in August when French traffic
is too jammed to kill anyone in. Maybe life just *seems* longer in
other countries.

Although you may live to a greater age overseas, don't get
cancer while you're doing it. Pipes gives the following figures.
The survival rate, five years after diagnosis of breast cancer, is
83.9 percent in the United States and 69.7 percent in Britain.
Americans are 35 percent more likely to survive colon cancer
than the British. And the prostate cancer survival rate is 91.9
percent in the United States, 73.7 percent in France, and 51.1
percent in the UK.

About a dozen countries have a live birth mortality rate
lower than America's. But don't fly there to be born if you're not

feeling well. America has sophisticated neonatal facilities that help preemies survive. This doesn't make America look better statistically. Those premature babies are still at high risk, and if they die they get counted as having died instead of being still-born. The United States adheres to the World Health Organization's definition of live birth, wherein the baby "breathes or shows any other evidence of life such as beating of the heart, pulsation of the umbilical cord, or definite movement of voluntary muscles." In Switzerland, says Pipes, "an infant must be at least 30 centimeters long at birth to be counted as living." In France, a live birth is not counted as such unless there is a "medical certificate stating that the child was born alive and"—here's the catch—"viable." In France and Belgium, "babies born at less than 26 weeks are automatically registered as dead."

America's health care spending may be excessive but one of the things we've bought with that excess is progress. The Cato Institute published a paper[33] by Glen Whitman and Raymond Raad (an economist and a physician, respectively) about America's role in making everybody—even foreigners—healthier. Among the figures cited were the number of Nobel Prizes for medicine and physiology (more rigorously vetted, I understand, than Nobel Prizes for peace). Between 1969 and 2008 Americans were awarded fifty-seven Nobels, seventeen more than were received by residents of the EU, Switzerland, Japan, Canada, and Australia combined. The U.S. National Institutes of Health has an annual budget of over $30 billion. Its counterparts in Europe receive a total of between $3 billion and $4 billion.

---

33. Policy Analysis no. 654, November 18, 2009, "Bending the Productivity Curve—Why America Leads the World in Medical Innovation."

Whitman and Raad also drew up a list of the twenty-seven most important innovations in medical diagonostics and therapeutics since 1975, drawing on 2001 research published in *Health Affairs* and updated with a survey of 225 primary care doctors. American scientists and physicians had a significant role in twenty of the inventions or advancements of technique including nine of the top-rated ten. Scientists and physicians from the EU and Switzerland made important contributions to fourteen innovations and only five of the top ten, despite western Europe being as wealthy as the United States and having almost 200 million more people. (The Netherlands leads the way in treating bong injuries.)

Health care in America is expensive not only because we're brilliant and hardworking, we're also old and fat. Sally Pipes reminds us that two-thirds of Americans are overweight, one-third of us are obese, one out of eight of us is over sixty-five, and by 2030, when the baby boom is fully installed in Nike brand walkers (slogan: "Just Do It—In Depends") the number will be one out of five.

An August 20, 2009, *New York Times* Web site article[34] about dying hospital patients stated—with a hint of healthy, young outrage that I'm not sure the *New York Times* is entitled to—that "a third of Medicare spending goes to patients with chronic illness in their last two years of life." Of course it does, that's when they're sick.

And, until we get sick, we're packing on the pounds. According to the Centers for Disease Control, weight-related medical bills accounted for $147 billion in health care spending in 2008. One hundred forty-seven billion is about half of what Medicare

---

34. "Months to Live—At the End, Offering Not a Cure but Comfort," by Anemona Hartocollis.

costs per year. My suggestion for health care reform is that we skip lunch and quit picking on sick people.

This was not President Obama's suggestion. President Obama suggested we find somebody to pick on that we hate even more than we hate sick people. With the clear-sighted political instincts for which the president is known, he suggested we pick on health insurance companies.

Everyone hates health insurance companies. Health insurance companies are always trying to get us to bet that something terrible will happen to us. And it's not like they're very good about paying up when they lose. "Your heart? Preexisting condition! Preexisting condition! You were *born* with a heart."

The president's idea was that the government get into the health insurance business to compete with private sector health insurance companies. The government would be just another competitor, like any other health insurance company. The only difference is that this competitor, being the government, has the legal monopoly on deadly force. This competitor has guns. What's another competitor, just like any other competitor, except it has guns? Suddenly, over at Blue Cross, it was like being the last legit trash hauler in New Jersey.

To put it another way, private sector health insurance companies are on the ducking stool. And President Obama has a scummy pool of numbers to dip them in. Forty-six million Americans, including nearly 8 million children, have no health insurance—figures that appeared in 2008 on the official Barack Obama Web site.[35] That's 15 percent of the population. But, if

---

35. WWW.BARACKOBAMA.COM/ISSUES/HEALTHCARE/.

you enjoy hating health insurance companies this is not a statistic you should look at too carefully the way Sally Pipes did in *Top Ten Myths*: "Myth Three: Forty-six Million Americans Can't Get Health Care." It seems that almost 10 million of the uninsured make more than $75,000 a year,[36] and 18 million make more than $50,000. These people should be able to buy some kind of health insurance or pay for their own medical treatment unless something extra terrible happens to them. The more so since these 28 million Americans tend to be young—nineteen- to twenty-nine-year-olds are one of the largest and fastest-growing segments of the uninsured population.[37] Another 10 million uninsured Americans turn out not to be Americans. That is, they aren't U.S. citizens.[38] Personally, I think when they get sick they should get as well as anyone else. But, technically, they're uninsured Canadians or uninsured Brazilians or uninsured chain-smoking Czech grad school habitués overstaying their student visas or whatever. Furthermore as many as 14 million uninsured Americans aren't uninsured. They qualify for the social insurance available under Medicare, Medicaid, and/or State Children's Health Insurance Program (SCHIP), but they have not

---

36. U.S. Census Bureau, "Income, Poverty, and Health Insurance Coverage in the United States: 2006." (P.S. Don't feel obligated to read all the footnotes in this chapter. They're here to show that I'm not pulling numbers out of your ear the way the Obama administration is.)

37. "Rite of Passage? Why Young Adults Become Uninsured and How New Policies Can Help, 2008 Update," Commonwealth Fund, New York, May 2008.

38. U.S. Census Bureau figures cited in "O's Health Rx: Cover Illegals," Dick Morris and Eileen McGann, *New York Post*, July 21, 2008. And, yes, it's the same Dick Morris. And, no, I wouldn't listen to him either if it weren't for the fact that, like any good conservative, I'm convinced that the Census Bureau is an all-knowing secret agency.

been enrolled.[39] Among these are a full 70 percent of uninsured children.[40]

Let's see, 10 million plus 18 million plus 10 million plus 14 million equals . . . Surely the official Barack Obama Web site could have produced even louder calls for hope and change if it had claimed "52 million Americans have no health insurance."

And there are those among that 52 million who do need help with their medical bills, people who make a decent wage but have chronic or degenerative conditions, who need expensive prescription drugs, who have sick children. And there's me. Only two years remain before I can drink (medicinally) from the Medicare tap, but what if, in the meantime, an unknown admirer were to send me a box of genuine Havana Montecristo no. 3s, putting me off my Nicorettes, and my health insurance company finds out?

There's something unhealthy, anyway, about framing a medical debate in terms of insurance. If your house catches fire do you call Allstate or the fire department? We'll figure out how to pay for the health care if we live. If we don't, fuck it.

The purpose of insurance is not to cure all that ails us but simply to prevent the plot of *The Merchant of Venice*. Antonio's covered by AIG and isn't worried about being short on cash to lend to Bassanio for wooing Portia. Tony can do a derivative swap and rake in the ducats. Shylock stays home watching

39. "The Uninsured in America," Blue Cross Blue Shield Association, Chicago, February 27, 2003.

40. "Reaching Eligible but Uninsured Children in Medicaid and SCHIP," Georgetown University Health Policy Institute, Center for Children and Families, March 2008.

interest rate fluctuations on the Bloomberg Business Canal. His daughter Jessica never gets a chance to go meshugana over Lorenzo (a schmuck, I'm telling you) and run off and charge a fortune on dad's Venetian Express card. And nobody's forced to become a mackerel snapper in Act 5. (True, Shylock never delivers his "If you prick us, do we not bleed?" solilioquy, which put an end to anti-Semitism in Europe for the next four hundred years. But everything comes with a price.)

Making everyone get health insurance has been tried in the United States, in Massachusetts, under the aegis of Republican governor Mitt Romney. As of July 1, 2007, everybody in the state had to either enroll in a state or federal program, if eligible, or buy a private insurance policy with no limit on annual benefits and a yearly maximum deductible of $5,000 per individual and $10,000 per family.

Massachusetts provides subsidies for private insurance policies purchased by families with incomes up to 300 percent of the poverty level. All employers with ten or more employees must provide health insurance for their workers or be assessed $295 per year per worker. And an individual who fails to get health insurance is charged $912 a year by the state. Carrots are available, in a stir-fry of small sticks.

Michael Tanner, a senior fellow at the Cato Institute, wrote a report[41] on what could be called the clinical test trial of universal insurance with Massachusetts as the clinic. Tanner concluded that it's all worked pretty much as expected—if you expect gov-

---

41. Cato Briefing Paper no. 112, June 9, 2009, "Massachusetts Miracle or Massachusetts Miserable."

ernment programs to work the way I expect them to. The insurance subsidies were intended to cost state taxpayers $725 mil-
lion a year. They cost more, as things that cost taxpayers usually
do. By mid-2008 Massachusetts was estimating that the health
insurance subsidies would cost $869 million in 2009 and $880
million in 2010. Income from assessments and penalties was
supposed to be $45 million in 2007 and $36 million in 2008.
There was no income from assessments and penalties in 2007
and $7 million in 2008. At the time of Tanner's report, the price
of Massachusetts health care reform in 2009 was projected to
be $225 million more than had been anticipated. State spending
on all health care programs had risen by 42 percent since 2006.
And health care reform was calculated to account for about a
third of the $1.3 billion 2008 state deficit.

The percentage of people without health insurance in Massachusetts did decline by 74 percent from 2006 to 2009. But
somehow 167,000 state residents were still left without health
insurance. And this is a state with only six and a half million
people, where those six and a half million have a greater per
capita disposable income than the people of any other state except Connecticut, New Jersey, and Wyoming.[42]

Meanwhile guess what Michael Tanner said about health
insurance premiums in Massachusetts? Or, if you prefer to get
your information from a source less biased toward free enterprise
than the Cato Institute, here is a headline and subhead from the
August 22, 2009, *Boston Globe*: "Bay State Premiums Highest in
Country: Rein in healthcare costs, Massachusetts urged."

------

42. New Jersey? That's what the U.S. Commerce Department's *Statistical Abstract of the United States* says. But New Jerseyites spent it all
on hair styling products. And what's with Wyoming? Did China buy it?

★   ★   ★

I couldn't have gotten into a medical school. I couldn't have
gotten into a veterinary school for goldfish. ("Flush twice and
call me in the morning.") At the college where I went all they
taught about health care was how to nurse a hangover. But I
do know something about going to hospitals and about other
people who go to hospitals and about the percentage of us people who go to hospitals needing medical treatment who get it,
which, in America, would be 100.

If you're sick or injured and you come to an emergency
room, they have to take you in. It's the law. That this doesn't
cost "health care providers" a fortune is not a law. Much of what
happens in the American health care industry would—in any
other business—be called shoplifting. Even in utopian Massachusetts, where the number of people without health insurance
dropped by 74 percent, the number of people who received un-
reimbursed care from the state's hospitals dropped by only 36
percent.[43]

I also know something about politics. The Affordable Health
Care for Americans Act, passed by the House of Representatives
on November 7, 2009, was 1,990 pages long. You could stand
on it to paint the ceiling. The entire U.S. Constitution can be
printed on eight pages. That's eight pages to run a whole country for 221 years versus four reams of government pig latin if
you slam your thumb in a car door.

No congressman had read this bill (even assuming they all
can read). And the busy president of the United States could
hardly have had time to do so. Not that this matters. Health care

---

43. Cato Briefing Paper no. 112.

reform is the *Sports Illustrated* Swimsuit Issue of politics. Beautiful, enticing, generously endowed legislation like this is not for reading. How it looks is what matters. From the neck up it can be as empty as you like.

There's only one thing about a government proposal of this complexity that we can be sure of: it won't work. No government proposal more complex than "This note is legal tender for all debts, public and private" ever works, and that one hasn't been working lately.

Also, doesn't anybody in Congress remember that Hillary Clinton has already been there with health care reform, seventeen years ago? A lot of people say that Hillary's health care reform plan almost destroyed Bill Clinton's first term. It certainly diminished Hillary's influence in the White House. Bill had to seek help from a different woman to almost destroy his second term.

There's a simpler way to make health care cheaper. Just make it worse. And politics can do that. Government-controlled health care will drive the best people out of the business. Who wants to spend all those years studying to be a doctor just to end up as a petty bureaucrat?

Someday we'll be wheeled in for a heart bypass operation and the surgeon will be the same person who's now behind the counter when we renew our registration at the Department of Motor Vehicles.

If we're not careful we'll get a health care system like they've got in Canada, a nation that's going broke from health care spending, even though Canada is a sparsely populated country with a shortage of gunshot wounds, crack addicts, and huge tort judgments. Anyway, what are Americans supposed to learn from a health care system devoted to removing pucks from goalie bridgework and treating sinus infections caused by trying to pronounce French vowels?

What we'll learn is to fix prices. Because that's all that political health care reform is—price fixing. Price fixing works so well in Cuba and North Korea. And in New York City rent-controlled apartments. Everybody knows how easy it is to find an inexpensive apartment in a nice neighborhood in New York.

And, by the way, why is price-fixing a public service when the government does it and a great big crime when Wall Street CEOs get together on a golf course?

Personally, I do smoke[44] and drink and my idea of exercise is getting up at 3 a.m. to go to the bathroom. I'm self-employed and I have to buy my own health insurance. I hardly need say that it comes with a high deductible and doesn't exactly cover everything. In fact, when my wife became pregnant, thirteen years ago, I discovered that my health insurance did not cover "normal pregnancy." In fairness, a pregnancy isn't an illness or an injury, and there's no such thing as it being an accident if you're Catholic.

We went to the hospital. My wife endured labor pains and the even bigger pain of having me there, uselessly hysterical. She gave birth to a beautiful baby girl, Muffin.

Mother and daughter were going fine. They were ready to be discharged. I went to the hospital's business administration office and said, "How much do I owe you?"

---

44. Montecristo no. 3s. There's a place in Toronto where you can buy them and they'll take the "Hecho en Cuba" cigar bands off and mail them to me in a box marked "Made in Honduras." And they're telling U.S. Customs the truth, the box *is* made in Honduras.

The woman at the desk stared at me, dumbfounded. She said, "Please complete all requisite insurance forms."

I said, "There's no insurance involved. Do you take credit cards, or would you like a check?"

She stared at me, dumbfounded.

I said, "Or, if you wait a moment, I can go to the bank and get cash."

Finally she said, "I have to get my supervisor."

The supervisor came out—and stared at me, dumbfounded. The supervisor had no idea how to handle this situation. From all appearances no one had ever before attempted to actually personally pay anybody for health care.

5

Climate Change

There's not a goddamn thing you can do about it. Maybe climate change is a threat, and maybe climate change has been tarted up by climatologists trolling for research grant cash. It doesn't matter. There are 1.3 billion people in China, and they all want a Buick. Actually, if you go more than a mile or two outside China's big cities, the wants are more basic. People want a hot plate and a piece of methane-emitting cow to cook on it. They want a carbon-belching moped, and some CO_2-disgorging heat in their houses in the winter. And air-conditioning wouldn't be considered an imposition, if you've ever been to China in the summer.

Now, I want you to dress yourself in sturdy clothing and arm yourself however you like—a stiff shot of gin would be my recommendation—and I want you to go tell 1.3 billion Chinese they can never have a Buick.

Then, assuming the Sierra Club helicopter has rescued you in time, I want you to go tell a billion people in India the same thing.

6

The End of the American Automobile Industry

To understand what doomed the American automobile we should give up on economics and turn to melodrama. Politicians, journalists, financial analysts, and other purveyors of banality have been looking at cars as if a convertible were a business. Fire the MBAs and hire a poet. The fate of Detroit isn't a matter of financial crisis, foreign competition, corporate greed, union intransigence, energy costs, or carbon emissions. It's a tragic romance—unleashed passions, titanic clashes, lost love, and wild horses.

Foremost are the horses. Cars can't be comprehended without horse sense. A hundred and some years ago Rudyard Kipling wrote a poem, "The Ballad of the King's Jest," in which an Afghan tribesman avers:

> *Four things greater than all things are,—*
> *Women and Horses and Power and War.*

Insert another "power" after the horse and the verse was as true in the suburbs of my boyhood as it was in the Khyber Pass.

Horsepower is not a quaint leftover of linguistics or a vague metaphoric anachronism. James Watt, father of the steam engine and progenitor of the industrial revolution, lacked a measurement for the movement of weight over distance in time, what we'd call energy. (What we'd call energy wasn't even an intellectual concept in the late eighteenth century, in case you think the 2008 financial crisis was history's most transformative moment.) Watt did research using draft animals and found that, under optimal conditions, a dray horse could lift 33,000 pounds one foot off the ground in one minute. Watt—the eponymous watt not yet existing—called this unit of energy "one horsepower." It is, by the way, equal to 746 watts. Thus your supposedly thrifty Honda Insight could illuminate a fair stretch of Broadway, causing enough harmful light pollution to offset the detrimental air pollution that you prevented by not buying a Cadillac Escalade.

In 1970 a Pontiac GTO (may the brand name rest in peace) had horsepower to the number of 370. In the time of one minute, for the space of one foot, it could move 12,210,000 pounds. And it could move those pounds down every foot of every mile of all the roads to the ends of the earth for every minute of every hour until the driver nodded off at the wheel. Forty years ago the pimply kid down the block, using $3,500 in saved-up soda-jerking money, procured might and main beyond the wildest dreams of Genghis Khan whose hordes went forth to pillage mounted upon less oomph than is in a modern leaf blower.

Probably Genghis Khan and the pimply kid were just looking for dates. Horses and horsepower alike are about status and being cool. A knight in ancient Rome was bluntly called "guy on horseback," *equesitis*. Chevalier means the same, as does Cavalier. Lose the capitalization on Cavalier and the dictionary says, "insouciant and debonair; marked by a lofty disregard of others' interests, rights, or feelings; high-handed, arrogant and supercilious." How cool is that? Then there are cowboys—always cool—and the U.S. cavalry that coolly comes to their rescue plus the proverbially cool-handed "Man on Horseback" to whom we turn in troubled times. (One reason that it's impossible to keep a straight face at anything Washington says is a mental picture of Barney Frank astride a prancing steed in the Lone Ranger manner, "Hi, ho, Executive Compensation! And away!")

Early witnesses to the automobile urged motorists to get a horse. But that, in effect, was what the automobile would do—get a horse for everybody. Once the Model T was introduced we all became Sir Lancelot, gained a seat at the Round Table, and were privileged to joust for the favors of fair maidens (at drive-in movies). The pride and prestige of a noble mount was vouchsafed to the common man. And woman too. No one ever tried to persuade ladies to drive sidesaddle with both legs hanging out the car door.

A car isn't necessarily cheaper than a horse, just cheaper than a horse you'd want. At about the time Henry Ford was peddling his Model T for $780, a yearling filly named Sceptre (admittedly with excellent racing bloodlines) sold at Newmarket for 10,000 guineas. In current U.S. dollars 10,000 guineas is . . . Let's just say that if ousted General Motors CEO Rick Wagoner—instead of a stallion called Ornament—had been the stud who sired Sceptre, it would have been GM telling the White House to get new management.

Cars, especially the cars of yore, were not reliable. But neither are horses, and at least with cars it isn't personal. Horses have complex psychologies and itty-bitty brains. Horses are like your adolescent children. Cars are like your computer.

The computer may be balky, slow, even worthless, but it never dresses itself all in black, gets every part of its keyboard pierced, screams that you just don't understand, and goes out and takes drugs and is brought home by the police at three in the morning. Actually, horses don't either. But you know what I mean.

Changing a tire on a car is no fun but it's easier than shoeing a horse. And you won't get kicked or bitten or have manure dumped on your head while you're changing a tire, unless you change it in a very bad neighborhood.

Cars may be put in dark, cramped, ill-ventilated places and left there for months and the ASPCA will not protest. For that matter cars may be thrashed in the street without raising public ire. (Although it's best if you own the car.)

Even when OPEC is doing its worst, cars are more efficient to fuel than horses. (Although a roll in the hay *is* preferable to a roll in the petroleum.)

And anyone who thinks that cars add to greenhouse gases and horses do not hasn't spent enough time behind a horse.

For the purpose of ennobling us schlubs, the car is better than the horse in every way. Even more advantageous than cost, convenience, and not getting kicked and smelly is how much easier it is to drive than to ride. I speak with feeling on this subject, having taken up riding when I was nearly sixty and having begun to drive when I was so small that my cousin Tommy had to lie on the transmission hump and operate the accelerator and the brake with his hands so that I could steer.

After the grown-ups had gone to bed Tommy and I shifted the Buick into neutral, pushed it down the driveway and out of earshot, started the engine, and toured the neighborhood. The sheer difficulty of horsemanship can be illustrated by what happened to Tommy and me next. Nothing. We maneuvered the car home, turned it off, and rolled it back up the driveway. (We were raised in the blessedly flat Midwest.) During our foray the Buick's speedometer reached 30. But 30 mph is a full gallop on a horse. Forget what you've seen of horse riding in movies. Possibly a kid who'd never been on a horse could ride at a gallop without killing himself. Possibly one of the Jonas Brothers could land an F-18 on a carrier deck.

Thus cars usurped the place of horses in our hearts. Once we'd caught a glimpse of a well-turned Goodyear, checked out the curves on the bodywork, and gaped at that swell pair of headlights, well, the old gray mare was not what she used to be. We embarked upon life in the fast lane with our new paramour. It was a great love story of man and machine. The road to the future was paved with bliss. Then we got married and moved to the suburbs.

Being away from central cities meant Americans had to spend more of their time driving. Over the years, away got farther away. Eventually this meant that Americans had to spend *all* of their time driving. The playdate was forty miles from the Chuck E. Cheese. The swim meet was forty miles from the cello lesson. The Montessori school was forty miles from the math coach. Mom's job was forty miles from Dad's job and the three-car garage was forty miles from both.

The car ceased to be object of desire and equipment for adventure and turned into office, rec room, communications hub, breakfast nook, and recycling bin—a motorized cupholder. Americans, the richest people on earth, were stuck in the confines of their Lexus crossover, squeezed into less space than tech-support call center employees in a Mumbai cubicle farm.

Never mind the six-bedroom, eight-bath, pseudo-Tudor with cathedral-ceilinged great room and thousand-bottle controlled climate wine cellar. It was a day's walk away.

We became sick and tired of our cars and even angry at them. Pointy-headed busybodies of the environmentalist, new urbanist, utopian type blamed the victim. They claimed the car had forced us to live in widely scattered settlements in the great wasteland of big box stores and the Olive Garden. If we would all just get on our twenty-speed derailleurs or hop a trolley, they said, America could become an archipelago of cozy gulags on the Portland, Oregon, model with everyone nestled together in the most sustainably carbon-neutral, diverse, and ecologically unimpactful way.

But cars didn't shape our existence; cars let us escape with our lives. We're way the heck out here in Valley Bottom Heights and Trout Antler Estates because we were at war with the cities. We fought rotten public schools, idiot municipal bureaucracies, corrupt political machines, rampant criminality, and all the pointy-headed busybodies. Cars gave us our dragoons and hussars, lent us speed and mobility, let us scout the terrain and probe the enemy's lines. And thanks to our cars, when we lost the cities we weren't forced to surrender, we were able to retreat.

But our poor cars paid the price. They were flashing swords beaten into dull plowshares. Cars became appliances. Or worse. Nobody's ticked off at the dryer or the dishwasher, much less the fridge. We recognize these as labor-saving devices. The car, on the other hand, seems to create labor. We hold the car responsible for all the dreary errands to which it needs to be steered. Hell, a golf cart's more fun. You can ride around in a golf cart with a six-pack, safe from Breathalyzers, chasing Canada geese on the fairways, and taking swings at gophers with a sand wedge.

We've lost our love for cars and forgotten our debt to them and meanwhile the pointy-headed busybodies have been exacting their revenge. We escaped the poke of their noses once, when we lived downtown, but we won't be able to peel out so fast the next time. In the name of safety, emissions control, and fuel economy, the simple mechanical elegance of the automobile has been rendered ponderous, cumbersome, and incomprehensible. One might as well pry the back off an iPod as pop the hood on a contemporary motor vehicle. An aging shade tree mechanic like myself stares aghast and sits back down in the shade. Or would if the car weren't squawking at me like a rehearsal for divorce. *You left the key in. You left the door open. You left the lights on. You left your dirty socks in the middle of the bedroom floor.*

I don't believe the pointyheads give a damn about climate change or gas mileage, much less about whether I survive a head-on with one of their tax-sucking mass transit projects. All they want is to make me hate my car. How proud and handsome would Bucephalus look or Traveller or Man O'War with seat and shoulder belts, air bags, 5 mph bumpers, and a maze of pollution control equipment under its tail?

And there's the end of the American automobile industry. When it comes to dull, practical, ugly things that bore and annoy me, Korean things cost less and have more cupholders.

The American automobile is—that is, was—never a product of Asian-style institutional industrialism. America's steel, coal, beer, beaver pelts, and PCs may have come from our business plutocracy, but American cars have been manufactured mostly by romantic fools. David Buick, Ransom E. Olds, Louis Chevrolet, Robert and Louis Hupp of the Hupmobile, the Dodge brothers, the Studebaker brothers, the Packard brothers, the Duesenberg brothers, Charles W. Nash, E. L. Cord, John North Willys, Preston Tucker, and William H. Murphy, whose Cadillac cars were designed by the young Henry Ford, all went broke making cars. The man who founded General Motors in 1908, William Crapo (really) Durant, went broke twice. Henry Ford, of course, did not go broke, nor was he a romantic, but judging by his opinions he certainly was a fool.

America's romantic foolishness with cars is finished, however, or nearly so. In the far boondocks a few good old boys haven't got the memo and still tear up the back roads. Doubtless the Department of Transportation is even now calculating a way to tap federal stimulus funds for mandatory OnStar installations to locate and subdue these reprobates. Among certain youthful Americans of Hispanic and Asian extraction there remains a fondness for Chevelle lowriders and hopped-up Honda "tuners." The pointy-headed busybodies have yet to enfold these youngsters in the iron-clad conformity of cultural diversity's embrace. Soon Wong and Juan will be expressing their creative energy in a more constructive way, planting bok choy in community gardens and decorating homeless shelters with murals of Che.

I myself have something old school under a tarp in the basement garage. I bet when my will has been probated, a child of mine will yank the dust cover and use the proceeds of the eBay sale to buy a mountain bike. Four things greater than all things are, and I'm pretty sure one of them isn't bicycles. There are those of us who have had the good fortune to meet with strength and beauty, with majestic force in which we were willing to trust our lives. Then a day comes, that strength and beauty fails, and a man does what a man has to do. I'm going downstairs to put a bullet in a V-8.

7

The Trade Imbalance

There is no such thing as a trade imbalance. Trade can't be out of balance because a balance is what trade is. Buyers and sellers decide that one thing is worth another. All free trade is balanced trade. Saying there's an imbalance in freely conducted trade is like saying there's an imbalance in freely conducted sex. It's like admitting you screwed some half-baked videographer who was hanging around your presidential campaign, and then claiming she had sex and you didn't. But you're not John Edwards.

There is no such thing as a trade deficit. It doesn't matter if America imports all its goods from China and exports nothing but pieces of paper. The Americans want the iPad and the Chinese want the handsome portraits of Benjamin Franklin. This is free trade. No coercion is involved. The only coercion existing in U.S./China trade comes in the form of import and export restrictions imposed by both countries to keep the trade from happening.

Nobody is making Americans buy Chinese goods. It's not like the Opium Wars of 1839–42 and 1856–60 when the British forced the Chinese to accept shipments of, shall we say, pharmaceutical exports. Maybe the Chinese will fight a war with America—the Consumer Electronics War of 2011, with Chinese gunboats cruising the fountains in America's malls. But it hasn't happened yet.

I look around my house and everything except the kids and dogs is made in China. And I'm not sure about the kids. They have brown eyes and small noses. All the Chinese got in return were those pieces of paper and an occasional 747 and some Yahoo software. Even if the software is illegally copied 1.3 billion times—and it has been; I've seen it for sale in Shanghai—China would appear to be getting the short end of the stick. Because here's another economic principle that's as inexorable as free trade: imports are good, exports are bad. Imports are an income, exports are an expense. Imports are Christmas morning, exports are January's Visa bill.

There's no such thing as a trade deficit, but there is such a thing as a current accounts deficit. The Chinese have decided to import money instead of things they can immediately enjoy— my black Lab would make quite a stir fry. China holds an enormous amount of U.S. money and we don't hold any of theirs. This worries America. I'll be damned if I know why.

The U.S. dollar is a promissory note from the Federal Reserve Bank, and it's not a promissory note that promises much. It's not backed by gold or silver or shares in Apple. If Hu Jintao brought a $100 bill to Washington and took the $100 bill to the Treasury Department—which he easily could do, if he could get a moment off from being annoyed and patronized by our president, because the Treasury building is right next door to the White House—all Hu could get for that $100 bill is a hundred dollars. He could get it in twenties. He could get it in tens. He could get it in shiny new dimes. But Treasury won't give anything to anybody for their American money except more American money.

China has the same kind of big, honking IOU that you've got in your Social Security account. (Hope all the Chinese don't decide to retire at the same time as us baby boomers!) When China holds an enormous amount of U.S. money, China is giving an interest-free loan to our Federal Reserve Bank.

Maybe American policy wonks are worried that China will suddenly spend all that cash and that this will somehow damage certain sectors of the American economy worse than America itself has managed to damage them. I've spent time in China and have eaten my share of its regional delicacies, and I will admit that if the Chinese spend all their U.S. dollars our pet shops will be stripped bare.

Or maybe America's policy wonks are worried that the current account deficit with China will cause the U.S. dollar to be devalued. In that case they can quit worrying about Chinese exports because every Hot Wheels car will be as expensive as if it had been hand-crafted by Louis Vuitton. This—in households such as mine where the annual demand for Hot Wheels cars is larger than a Toyota recall—will cause rampant inflation. Then the policy wonks can worry about that.

One more thing the wonks worry about is that the renminbi is too cheap, that in order to make Chinese exports more attractive the Chinese government is artificially keeping the value of China's currency too low. It is. And, when it comes to buying exports, the other fellow's currency can't *be* too low. It's like the importer has gone to a Hollywood real estate agent who says, "There's a house in Beverly Hills. The price is five million dollars. But my client will take five million Mexican pesos instead."

★   ★   ★

Has Chinese economic development cost American workers their jobs? Sure. That's the price of progress. The invention of fire cost Cro-Magnon workers their jobs—all those people you paid to sit on you to keep you warm. But no American politician, whether elected, appointed, or squatting on the *New York Times* editorial board, is going to go on *Hardball* and tell us that when we lose our job, due to some guy in Guangzhou being willing to do it for $145 a month, it's because what we did wasn't worth a shit.

When you're doing something that isn't worth a shit (and I speak as a print journalist), you've got two choices. Either you can do something that *is* worth a shit or you can try to make everyone else do something that's as shit worthless as what you do. You can be Chinese or you can be French. You can build cars or you can burn them in the suburbs of Paris. We don't want the Chinese doing things that aren't worth a shit such as crossing the Yalu in hordes the way they did during the Korean War or wading the Formosa Strait to belatedly settle Chiang Kai-shek's hash in Taiwan. Let's keep them busy making money.

Consider that the Chinese are doing our work for us, making the things we want. Personally, I'd love to outsource my work to some underpaid political barf artist in Beijing. And the Chinese are giving us zero percent financing on the money we owe them for doing our work. On top of that the Chinese are underwriting America's national debt. Somebody has to. Between the bailout and the stimulus and the president's lies about freezing spending and the Republicans' lies about helping him and the fact that we've all run through our savings, which we didn't have any of to begin with, because we're out of a job, *America* certainly isn't going to do anything about America's national debt.

Consider also the parable of Japan in the 1980s. Japan kept giving America radios, TVs, stereos, and cars and we kept giving Japan money. The Japanese didn't want anything America produced except Bo Derek, and we didn't even produce the valuable part—the silicon part—of that. So the Japanese decided, instead of buying anything Americans made, they'd buy America itself. They bought office complexes, hotels, resorts. They bought Pebble Beach. They bought Rockefeller Center. The Japanese bid up the price of American real estate. There was a bubble. The bubble did what bubbles do. And by the 1990s America had all the radios, TVs, stereos, and cars, *and* America had Pebble Beach and Rockefeller Center, *and* America had all the money too. The Japanese had stuck their economy in a place where the rising sun never shines.

If our wonks are going to worry, they should worry about China. The Chinese have—let us not forget Tiananmen Square—worse politics than we do. If China can't keep its economic progress going, the political consequences could be dire. Gang of Four: The Adventure Continues. Great Leap Backward.

Meanwhile, in view of China's trade policies, what should American policy be? We might try a policy of good manners. "Thank you, China, for doing all the shit work."

8

Gun Control

Gun ownership is crucial to the preservation of American freedoms. We may have to shoot Democrats. It happened in 1861 and it could happen again. Just kidding. Sort of. But there are other important arguments in favor of gun ownership. What with the economy being like it is, I call my .38 Special "the MasterCard of the future."

True, guns take a dreadful toll in killings and other heinous crimes. The historical term for this is war. Compared to the amount of bloody carnage produced by men in uniforms carrying guns, America's criminals, psychopaths, hotheads, and men "mistaking" their wives' return from Bingo for home invasions might as well be armed with water balloons.

I was going to tally the number of wars that America has been involved in, but somewhere between Shays's Rebellion and the Barbary Coast wars I lost count, and I was only four years into the nineteenth century. Countries have always had wars. But this country is a democracy. All our wars have been conducted by people elected or appointed through our democratic political system.

Guns don't kill people, votes do. If we were serious about reducing American deaths and property damage we wouldn't be arguing about gun control, we'd be arguing about vote control.

Most states already have restrictions on felons being allowed to have a vote (although they are woefully behindhand on felonious-type candidates being allowed to *get* a vote). Nonetheless the percentage of Americans with a vote has proliferated, doubling since the ratification of the Nineteenth Amendment in 1920. America now has almost one vote for every U.S. citizen over the age of eighteen. Nearly half of all Americans with a vote have used it in past elections, often with tragic results. Think of the prominent Americans cut down in their prime by the vote: Herbert Hoover, Adlai Stevenson, Barry Goldwater, Hubert Humphrey, Gerald Ford, Michael Dukakais, George H. W. Bush, Bob Dole, John McCain, and (if you're counting popular vote) George W. Bush in 2000. The current president of the United States has been threatened by votes aimed at him in Virginia, New Jersey, and Massachusetts. Virtually all of America's votes are unregulated. Even in the few jurisdictions where strict vote control exists, such as Boston, it often goes unenforced. Witness the loss of Martha Coakley's political life.

Of course no one wants to ban votes. Votes should remain available for sporting and recreational purposes. But certain types of votes need to be prohibited. "Assault votes," for example, where the only purpose of the vote is to inflict harm on others. One thinks of the angry, impulsive voters of California's eighth congressional district senselessly returning Nancy Pelosi to the House of Representatives.

Although we hear a great deal about electoral candidates paying high prices for votes, a greater danger is to be found in cheap and unreliable votes, the so-called First-Tuesday-in-November Nothing Specials. These should be outlawed, as should the importation of low-quality arms (and legs) from foreign sources. Flimsy breechloaders such as Patrick Kennedy, late of Rhode Island, come to mind. And extra penalties should be meted out for crimes committed with a vote such as the federal budget.

The League of Women Voters, Rock the Vote, leaders of various get-out-the-vote campaigns, and other members of the well-financed pro-vote movement would have us believe that the "right to vote" is enshrined in American law. But constitutional scholars, especially Judge Robert Bork after a couple martinis, agree that there is no absolute constitutional right to vote. The Fifteenth, Nineteenth, Twenty-fourth, and Twenty-sixth amendments merely stipulate that possession of a vote cannot be denied on the basis of race, gender, failure to pay poll tax, or having pierced eyebrows, neck tattoos, listening to Adam Lambert, tweeting incessantly, and wearing Uggs. Otherwise, vote regulations are left to the states, with the Fourteenth Amendment requiring only that, to the extent states limit vote holding, their congressional representation shall be proportionally reduced. If the state of South Carolina had limited vote use to those whose spouses had been propositioned by the governor, the whole gruesome Mark Sanford scenario may never have transpired.

In fact, contrary to supposed constitutional prohibition of vote control, every state in the Union practices voter registration. From there it is a small step to requiring background checks and sensible waiting periods. (Al Gore would have survived to become a venerated ex-president—and UN special envoy to the North Pole—if Palm Beach County voters had had a chance to pause and reflect and remember who Pat Buchanan was before using their votes.)

Every vote should carry a serial number so that responsibility for harmful employment of votes can be traced. Concealed votes should be illegal. No secure society is possible when we do not know which of the people we encounter in public places might suddenly vote for Newt Gingrich.

And votes must be kept out of the hands of children. Nothing is more tragic in American life than parents who have suffered the loss of their Direct TV due to careless youthful voting on program selection. No episode of *The Suite Life of Zack and Cody* can ever replace a National League playoff. Childproof remotes are an immediate imperative.

I hope all concerned Americans will join me in this worthy, bipartisan campaign to make America vote-safe.

Campaign Finance Reform

People who think good thoughts have been denouncing the grievous effects of unfettered campaign spending in the United States since before the States were united. In 1759, while running for a seat in the Virginia House of Burgesses, George Washington was criticized for serving a quart and a half of liquor to each voter. This should tell us something about the relationship between electoral corruption and optimal political outcomes. Drunk as monkeys though they were, Virginians elected George Washington.

The most recent campaign spending issue causing thinkers of good thoughts to think their heads off is a January 21, 2010, ruling by the U.S. Supreme Court. The Supreme Court justices decided—never mind what they'd decided before—that corporations, labor unions, trade associations, and organizations of writhing, naked political bedfellows can spend as much as they like trying to get elections to go to hell.

Now everyone's in a tizzy, including the Supreme Court justices. In the minority opinion, Justice John Paul Stevens wrote, "While American democracy is imperfect, few outside the majority of this court would have thought its flaws included a dearth of corporate money in politics."

In the majority opinion, Justice Anthony Kennedy wrote, "Governments are often hostile to speech, but under our law and our tradition it seems stranger than fiction for our government to make . . . political speech a crime."

"Today's Supreme Court decision . . . is a disaster for the American people," said Fred Wertheimer, founder of Democracy 21, a reform group that often gets called pinko.

"This is a great day for the First Amendment," said Brooklyn Law School professor Joel M. Gora, a longtime lawyer for the ACLU, a reform group that often gets called pinko.

Voices of moderation were heard, such as that of Christopher Cotton, assistant professor of economics at the University of Miami: "Academic research has not found much of a link between increases in a candidate's campaign spending and increases in the probability of the candidate winning the election." Oh, shut up, voices of moderation were told.

President Obama called the Supreme Court ruling "a major victory for big oil, Wall Street banks, health insurance companies . . ." At which point he seemed to run out of kinds of corporations that Americans are ticked at. ". . . and other powerful interests," he said. Surely, if the president had thought for a moment, he would have added, ". . . those people who call in the middle of dinner and want you to switch cell phone services."

The case that came before the Supreme Court, *Citizens United v. Federal Election Commission,* did not in fact have its origin in anything so straightforward and sensible as, for example, JP-Morgan Chase wanting to buy Barney Frank's congressional seat and sell it on NASDAQ. As often happens, the Supreme Court made a big constitutional decision due to a small group of nutters. A nonprofit organization, Citizens United, made a documentary titled, *Hillary: The Movie,* which was intended to be released on cable TV during the 2008 presidential primaries. The film—I quote the *Economist*—"portrays Mrs. Clinton as a lying, power-hungry viper." The Federal Election Commission invoked the McCain-Feingold campaign finance legislation and forbade public showing of *Hillary: The Movie* within thirty days of a Democratic primary. (Even though I, as an ununited citizen, was free to go on cable TV and shout at Citizens United, "How come you're so soft on Hillary!") Citizens United was threatened with large fines and jail terms of up to five years if the FEC ruling was violated. This sounds like the kind of thing that Alexander Hamilton, in *The Federalist Papers* number 84, had warned that a First Amendment could lead to, and the Supreme Court decided not to go there.

Lefty nutters were involved as well. Emily's List had brought a similar, if less publicized, case against the FEC in the District of Columbia Circuit Court and won. The FEC did not appeal the judgment, and in December 2009 the Justice Department announced that it didn't feel very appealing either. The federal judge who ruled in favor of Emily's List had been an associate White House counsel in the George W. Bush administration when the Bush administration strengthened regulations on spending by groups like Emily's List and Citizens United. The attorney representing Emily's List, Bob Bauer, went on to be appointed as White House counsel by Barack Obama. The Supreme Court justices had probably heard about all this.

Under progressive, populist, public-spirited Democratic presidential administrations, campaign finance reform acts were passed in 1939, 1943, 1947, and 1967. But wait. Under regressive, plutocratic, special-interest-dominated Republican presidential administrations, campaign finance reform acts were passed in 1883, 1907, 1910, 1911, 1925, 1971, 1974, and 2002. No less a mossback than Senator Barry Goldwater once co-sponsored a bill to cap donations by political action committees.

There are all sorts of thinkers of good thoughts. Neither liberal nor conservative politicians seem to be able to resist the temptation to stand as mighty sequoias of rectitude amid the lowly underbrush of campaign fund-raising. Still, as ace political strategist Ralph Reed once said, "Money is like water down the side of the mountain. It will find a way to get around the trees."

Those of us who do not think good thoughts any more often than we have to may wonder, simply, "Does campaign finance reform work?" We can let history be the judge. (I'm a great fan of "let history be the judge," figuring that by the time Shelby Foote gets around to deciding whether or not I flunked the Breatha-lyzer test I'm history.) The strictest laws to date concerning electoral donations were passed in the McCain-Feingold Bipartisan Campaign Reform Act of 2002, which went into effect after the 2002 elections. It had long been illegal for corporations, unions, trade associations, and so forth to donate directly to a political candidate. But McCain-Feingold banned so-called soft money donations as well—money given to the Republican, Democratic, or Whatever Party rather than to a particular candidate from that party. McCain-Feingold also prohibited political advertising by corporations, unions, etc., if the ads even mentioned a specific candidate, pro or con. And McCain-Feingold limited most of the rest of the material help that might be given to a political candidate. You could (the legislation originally stipulated) give a candidate $5,000 if you were a political action committee,

$5,000 if you were a political party, or $2,000 if you were a human. You could still display a yard sign, assuming your home owner's association allowed it. And Senator McCain and Senator Feingold never were able to figure out a way to prevent rich candidates from supporting themselves. Thus the first result of the McCain-Feingold Act was to cause Washington's wise men to say, "The only way to get elected now is to have a huge Rolex or a huge Rolodex."[45]

Much of the McCain-Feingold balloon of good thoughts has been punctured by the 2010 Supreme Court ruling. But we still have the examples of the pre-McCain-Feingold 2000 and 2002 federal elections versus the post-McCain-Feingold 2004 federal elections to show us how—if not whether—campaign finance reform works.

In 2004, for the first time in history, the average cost of an election victory in the House of Representatives exceeded $1 million. The cost of victorious Senate elections rose by 47 percent from 2002 to 2004. Total spending on presidential, Senate, and House races was almost $4 billion in 2004 compared to approximately $3 billion in 2000. So the McCain-Feingold Act was a failure. Unless it wasn't. After all, Americans were 33 percent more politically involved in 2004 than they had been in 2000, if we measure involvement in dollars. And the fact that an extra billion in campaign funds was raised, despite onerous new restrictions on fund-raising, is proof of the ingenuity and flexibility that makes American democracy so—corruptly—successful.

Has the Supreme Court made this electoral bettering or worsening worse or better? We won't know until there's been a

---

45. N.B. to those under thirty: a primitive analog address and phone number search engine.

great festival of litigation. For the moment corporations, unions et al. are still prevented from giving directly to candidates, and PAC, party, and individual donations remain capped. But a few things are clear. Fortunately we don't have to rely on good thoughts to know what they are. Some real thinking has been done. On the same day that the Supreme Court decision was announced, Republican election lawyer Ben Ginsberg and other scary-smart people at the lobbying firm of Patton Boggs circulated a memo titled "A drastically altered landscape."

The Patton Boggs conclusions: Republicans are about to get swamped because of an "extremely well-funded union effort that gives over 98 percent of its funds to Democrats." Democrats are sunk because "Democrats see the size of corporate treasuries compared to unions and believe they are about to get swamped." Political parties are on the rocks because "with the limits on the amounts and sources of funds they can accept the parties will be bit players compared to outside groups." Nutters are washed up because 527s (the groups named after the section of the tax code that allows nutters to go nuts tax free) have "been rendered obsolete." (Say bon voyage to nasty TV ads calling a decorated war veteran presidential candidate a swift boat goldbrick and hysterical Web sites claiming that George W. Bush's father was snapped by paparazzi lolling topless on the deck of King Faisal's yacht.) Candidates are rudderless because "limits . . . on the size of contributions to candidates place them at a significant disadvantage compared to corporations and unions, [therefore] controlling the issues they want to run on will become a real challenge." And candidates running against incumbents are lost at sea because "corporations' political giving tends to be incumbent heavy."

Here is something that makes Republicans, Democrats, political parties in general, nutters, politicians, and would-be politicians walk the plank. One begins to see the Supreme Court's
point.

The situation reminds me of a debate about term limits that
Cato president Ed Crane and I have been having for twenty-two
years. Ed favors term limits. I say, "It's a good thought, Ed. But
do you want a dog that knows where the bones are buried, or do
you want a dog that will dig up the *whole* yard?"

To which Ed replies, "P.J., there's one thing I can tell you
about term limits. Every politician hates them."

It's an argument I can't refute.

Is there too much money in politics? There are some 230 million
Americans of voting age. The 2008 presidential campaigns spent
about $1.4 billion. Would you have sold your vote for $6.16? (I
would have, if I could have simultaneously voted against Joe
Biden and Sarah Palin, but Ron Paul never coughed up the six
bucks. Besides, Ron, if you're going to be as libertarian as all
that, you need to get some tattoos or something.)

Do the possessors of money wield too much influence at
the polls? They do at the mall, doubtless likewise in voting
booths. Yet the telecommunications industry, comprising some
of America's richest corporations, is constantly pestered by government regulatory agencies while agriculture, making up 2.3
percent of the GDP, is lavishly subsidized. Government is so
inefficient that it can't even get bribe-taking right.

What is the alternative to private financing of political campaigns? Only one alternative exists. Under a system of public financing of political campaigns, people trying to change the government would have to go to the government to get the money to try to change the government. Something a little East German about that?

We should ignore who gives what to whom and vote for candidates on the basis of their ideas and actions. Like that would help. The perpetuation of slavery, the exile and extermination of American Indians, and the passage of Jim Crow laws weren't policies carried out at the behest of malefactors of great wealth. These ideas and actions had the support of ordinary voters—the individual, small-donor, John Q. Public members of the electorate whose will is supposed to be upheld and protected by campaign finance reform.

10

Terrorism

The law and the jury are a free country's Eucharist, the body and blood of liberty. By attempting to put "9/11 mastermind" Khalid Sheikh Mohammed on criminal trial with civilian jurors, the Obama administration is using communion wafers as Kleenex and giving an enema with the sacramental wine.

Khalid Sheikh Mohammed was arrested in Pakistan in 2003. Pakistan is not exactly a free country, but it likes to make a show of freedom's outward forms such as laws and judges. But, fond as Pakistan is of legal formalities, these were obviously ridiculous in the case of Khalid who was handed over to the CIA.

Khalid had been a known enemy of the global commonwealth years before the destruction of the World Trade Center towers. He'd been indicted on terrorism charges in U.S. federal court in 1996, as a result of a failed conspiracy to explode twelve commercial airlines over the Pacific. Khalid had been in the Philippines, plotting this carnage with his nephew Ramzi Yousef, who had directed the 1993 bombing of the World Trade Center. Khalid fled to Qatar. America requested his arrest. Khalid "eluded" Qatari authorities despite working for Qatar's Ministry of Electricity and Water in a country with exactly two airports and a population smaller than Tulsa, Oklahoma's. Khalid moved to Afghanistan where he palled around with fellow immigrant newcomer Osama bin Laden.

Khalid confessed to planning the 9/11 attacks and to any number of other things including assisting Ramzi Yousef in 1993; sending shoe bomber Richard Reid on his bootless mission; organizing the suicide bombings of a nightclub in Bali and a hotel in Mombasa; making plans to blow up the Panama Canal, Heathrow Airport, Big Ben, NATO headquarters, the New York Stock Exchange, U.S. embassies in Indonesia, Japan, and Australia, and Israeli embassies in Austria, India, the Philippines, and Azerbaijan; devising a way to destroy the Sears Tower in Chicago with flaming fuel trucks; sketching out a post–9/11 "second wave" of attacks on U.S. landmarks such as the Empire State Building and the Sears Tower again; plotting to assassinate Pakistani president Pervez Musharraf, Bill Clinton, Pope John Paul II, and Jimmy Carter; and contriving an assault on a Sumatran oil company "owned"—the Pentagon quoted Khalid as saying—"by the Jewish former secretary of state Henry Kissinger."

Khalid also confessed to murdering *Wall Street Journal* reporter Daniel Pearl. According to the Pentagon, he said, "I decapitated with my blessed right hand the head of the American Jew, Daniel Pearl, in the city of Karachi, Pakistan. For those who would like to confirm, there are pictures of me on the Internet holding his head." A simple "I did it" would have sufficed.

A January 29, 2010, article on the *New York Times* Web site states, "The decision on how to prosecute Mr. Mohammed has been particularly difficult because his defense lawyers are expected to argue that he was illegally tortured by the Central

Intelligence Agency during his confinement, tainting any evidence gathered from his interrogations. Documents have shown that the CIA used waterboarding—a controlled drowning technique—against Mr. Mohammed 183 times in March 2009."

The problem with this line of defense is how the hell would it occur to a CIA agent, no matter how bored he was with dipping Khalid's head in the sink, to ask anybody to confess to an assassination attempt on Jimmy Carter? I wasn't even certain that Carter was still alive. In fact, during the Winter Olympics, I misunderstood a news broadcaster saying, "a Georgian luger has died" and was sure it was Carter. Plus I'll bet the CIA didn't even know that Israel had an embassy in Azerbaijan (and probably needed to have Khalid spell Azerbaijan for them). Furthermore I'm having trouble picturing Henry Kissinger as a wildcatter in Sumatra.

My father-in-law is a retired FBI agent. He has a lot of friends from the Bureau who've been involved in plenty of interrogations. I asked one of these former agents about waterboarding.

"Heck, yes!" he said. "Waterboard him six ways from Sunday! Waterboard the dickens out of him!"

"But," I said, "is waterboarding a good way to get information out of somebody?"

"Information?" said the former agent. "Oh, no. The way you get information out of somebody is you pretend to be his friend. But I say waterboard him till his feet leak!"

So my suggestion to the government attorneys suffering from indecision about how to prosecute Khalid Sheikh Mohammed is to sidle up and get tight and discover whether he's really an evil mastermind, and, if he's just bragging, really throw the book at him.

★   ★   ★

It's tempting to claim that terrorists are the result of the ideal-istic rationalism that has been the creeping nemesis of politics for three hundred years. And terrorism is indeed the product of trying to make politics an idea-driven process. Ideas become so important that you kill people for them. The historian A. J. P. Taylor was a great left-wing baloney monger of the rationalist school, but he did have his moments of sense. In the introduc-tion to a book of laudatory essays on the European revolutions of 1848, he said, "Reason formulates universal principles and is therefore intolerant . . . Decisions between rival reasons can be made only by force."[46]

Terrorism happens when someone gets to be so overformu-lated with his universal principles that he uses force on people who never had an idea in their lives. Here is the reasoning, as explained by Richard E. Rubenstein in *Alchemists of Revolution: Terrorism in the Modern World*[47]: "To sow terror among the clique of power, which would expose its weakness, provoke brutal over-reaction, and inspire mass support of radical change." (Whether waterboarding Khalid Sheikh Mohammed 183 times is brutal overreaction or whether giving him a presumption of innocence and a public defender is an exposure of weakness, I leave to the reader.)

And here are the conclusions reached with the terrorist's reasoning, as put forth in the 1849 essay "Murder"[48] written by

---

46. *The Opening of an Era, 1848: A Historical Symposium,* ed. François Fejtö, New York, 1966.

47. New York, 1987.

48. *The Terrorism Reader,* ed. Walter Laqueur, New York, 1978.

one of the first modern theorists of terror, German radical Karl Heinzen.

> The greatest benefactor of mankind will be he who makes it possible for a few men to wipe out thousands . . . underground rooms full of fulminating silver [that] can blow whole towns into the air, complete with their 100,000 murderous slaves . . . To have a conscience with regard to the murdering of reactionaries is to be totally unprincipled . . . The man who would not joyfully give up his own life for the satisfaction of putting a million barbarians into their coffins carries no Republican heart within his breast.

Heinzen ran off to the United States when the European revolutions of 1848 came a cropper. He lived in Boston (the Berkeley of its day), which he called "the only civilized place in America," and he caused no further trouble. (There are probably men bankrolled by Al-Qaeda who've been sent to the United States with similar results.)

As indicated by the "Republican heart" that Heinzen mentioned, terrorism is not, however, just a product of left-wing politics and its offshoot fascism. Terrorists, like killjoys (but literally), can be found among conservatives. The earliest terrorists that we know of[49] were the Jewish Zealots, a zealously conservative bunch. The Romans were the secular humanist progressives of 73 AD, and the Romans were as baffled by the events at Masada as we are by the events in Pakistan's tribal areas.

---

49. Certainly not the first, but I follow the textbook *Understanding Terrorism,* by James M. Poland, of California State University, Sacramento, 2004.

The Assassins, who terrorized the Islamic world for two centuries at the beginning of the previous millennium, were a Shi'ite sect determined to return the rule of Islam to the descendants of the Prophet Muhammad. They were legitimists, like the devotees of nineteenth-century French Bourbonism, except not silly.

Niccolò Machiavelli was a Bill Clinton in his politics, with no principles right or left. Given the clear-sighted political instincts that such morality purblind people have, Machiavelli, in *The Discourses*, offered both radical and conservative briefs for terrorism. New political leaders, full of new ideas, should frighten everybody: "Make the rich poor and the poor rich . . . as well as to build new cities, to destroy those already built, and to move the inhabitants from one place to another far distant from it; in short, to leave nothing . . . intact."[50] Meanwhile, political leaders who wish to keep everything perfect, the way it was in the good old days, should do the same: "In regard to this, those who governed the state of Florence from 1434 to 1494 used to say that it was necessary to reconstitute the government every five years; otherwise it was difficult to maintain it; where by 'reconstituting the government' they meant instilling men with that terror and that fear with which they had instilled them when instituting it."[51]

No matter if the hyperidealist wants to go forward, backward, or stay in one place, terror works for him. Sergey Nechayev was a Russian nihilist or anarchist or some damn thing, author of *Catechism of a Revolutionary*,[52] one of those excretions of the czarist era that reemerges periodically among political heathens,

---

50. Book I, chapter 26.

51. Book III, chapter 1.

52. *The Terrorist Reader.*

like *The Protocols of the Elders of Zion*. Nechayev's only action of note was to have a young student, whom he considered to be a traitor to his revolutionist "society," killed and to thereby provide the plot for Dostoyevsky's novel *The Possessed*. But Nechayev, in common with most provokers of civic horror, was a deep thinker.

> Our society has only one aim . . . the total emancipation and happiness of the people . . . But, convinced that their emancipation and the achievement of this happiness can be realized only by means of an all-destroying popular revolution, our society will employ all its power and all its resources in order to promote an intensification and an increase in those calamities and evils which must finally exhaust the patience of the people and drive them to a popular uprising.[53]

The patience of the people is exhausted. The uprising should consist of Khalid Sheikh Mohammed climbing thirteen steps to a scaffold and putting his head into (Khalid has a degree in mechanical engineering from North Carolina Agricultural and Technical State University and will know what this means) a "short control loop."

---

53. Quoted in *Alchemists of Revolution*.

11

Foreign Policy

I had expected the current administration to be wrong about foreign policy. I hadn't expected it to be pathetic. This administration seems to be made up of whiney, wavering scolds; insecure, self-righteous bumblers; and pious frauds lecturing humanity on morals while possessing no whit of moral understanding themselves. Their approach to international relations is vain, testy, inconsistent, and meddlesome, by turns too skeptical and too credulous, too permissive and too controlling, too understanding and too obtuse. In its conduct of foreign policy this administration is acting like . . . me.

I behave exactly the same way with my family. The problem is, we're talking about a much larger family here. I am the head of the O'Rourkes. America is the head of the family of nations.

"The Family of Nations" is something I suspect that most members of President Obama's foreign policy team believe in. It's a fatuous idea, and hackneyed—unless we hate our family. And we should. The Family of Nations is a terrible kinship group. As the eldest semisolvent unincarcerated O'Rourke male in his right mind, I know of what I speak. Not that I hate *my* family, of course. But none of my family has atomic bombs.

The Family of Nations is a wrongheaded notion but not without its value as an analytical tool if the countries of the world are considered as members of a large, raucous, conniving, belligerent Irish clan, some of them inebriated with fanaticism, others just inebriated, and all of them asking each other—as the O'Rourke motto goes—"Is this a private fight or can anyone join in?"

I suppose the more idealistic among our foreign policy elite imagine that someday there will be a stirring display of clan loyalty with factious elders of the tribe uniting everyone in the face of a common foe, such as global warming. The Family of Nations will coalesce to battle a mutual adversary, and the earth will be invaded by flying monkeys from Neptune. Until the winged apes with ray guns arrive, arrangements such as the UN, the WTO, the World Bank, and the Copenhagen Treaty on Climate Change will end up like a wedding reception at the Friends of Hibernia Hall or a wake at the Shamrock & Pig. (Pin your hopes on the wake, one less bloody nose.)

So how is America doing as patriarch in the household of humankind? One way to gauge our standing with the relatives is: Do they all go to us asking for money? We're good on this count. We've displayed an open hand to all who come our way, and we've dropped hints that we'll even travel to them to provide largesse, be they as far away as Tehran or Pyongyang. We're the soul of generosity, as have been all Americans who've come before us since Woodrow Wilson (except for Calvin Coolidge, the piker). Never mind that the money belongs to our rich, nervous, high-strung aunt, the American economy. Auntie Con has been suffering from a bit of a breakdown lately. We've gotten our hands on her power of attorney and we're frittering away her wealth.

I hope we're not expecting our distant relations to be grateful. A hundred years ago when foreign aid was unthought of (except as tribute or bribe) we were a respected and admired country. After a century of philanthropy everyone hates our guts.

This should tell us something about spoiling the kids. That red-haired stepson Hamas, for example. We don't "bring him to the table" with some invitation to come home for the holidays (especially if the holiday is the anniversary of 9/11). We tell the little jerk to quit playing with his rocket launcher toys and get a job.

And why, by the way, are we so down on smart, hardworking nephew Izzy? Are we jealous because he's successful in real estate? All those settlements on the West Bank—his housing market investments are doing a lot better than ours.

Or is there something in us that can't resist a quarrel with our nearest and dearest. Plenty of other states and territories have been that way, historically. Look at the Yugoslav clan. We're always hardest on our own. I mean, it wasn't very nice the way we treated that gal who's married to America's ex, Bill. Sure, nobody likes her. But first we give Hillary a big secretary of state job in the family firm. And then we send her lothario of a husband, instead of her, to rescue the hot newscaster chicks in North Korea. That was just mean.

We should spend more time dealing with the threats to a quiet life at home. There's our troubled boy Iraq. Are we going to make sure he gets the help he needs? Or are we going to go all "tough love" and to hell with him?

Then there's Afghanistan, upon whom we once so doted, standing on our doorstep holding in her arms a tiny illegitimate democracy wrapped in a *hijab*. Will we send her away? Will we tell her to go see the social workers over at Taliban?

What about crazy cousin Pakistan? She's been on suicide watch since 1947. She was a mess long before she started fighting with her live-in boyfriend Al Qaeda, a convicted felon.

Estranged foster child Iran is off his medications again. How long before this bipolar psychopath pulls a Columbine among our slow-learner kin in the special education class that is Europe?

Speaking of Europe, Russia's out on parole, drunk, unemployed, and likely to kill some folks next door again soon.

Doddering grandma Great Britain still manages on her own. But are we going to help her with her shopping for antiterror commitment and her cleaning up of lefty defeatists? Are we going to keep this special relationship special? Or are we going to stick Gram into EU assisted living?

And all those work-shy layabouts on the Continent, don't we understand that they're good-for-nothings? But we want that branch of the family tree's approval so badly that our president wears his Nobel Peace Prize medal to bed at night.

Meanwhile our cousins down south are total screw-ups. The Honduras marriage is on the rocks—we're talking "burning bed syndrome." And all we do is suggest they seek counseling.

We know we should call the cops on Venezuela but we don't have the nerve. And we think a little flattery and a gift basket will convince Cuba not to strap her children in the infant seats of Marxism and roll the minivan of dictatorship into the Caribbean Sea.

Yes, as we can see, the Family of Nations concept is useful. One wishes one could say the same for the rest of the family.

Maybe we should tell the Family of Nations that America's getting a divorce. Mutual incompatibility will serve as grounds, or we can make a case that the world is guilty of abuse and neglect. There's incontrovertible evidence. The property settlement is a simple matter. America keeps everything she brought to the matrimonial union, leaving the respondent party with zilch. Visitation rights will be determined by a mediation panel—the army, the navy, the air force, and the marines. As for support payments, we have retained, as counsel for the plaintiff, Helen Wait. If alimony is desired, go to Helen Wait.

Let's give up on the Family of Nations notion and content ourselves merely with living in the "Neighborhood of Nations"— the bad neighborhood of nations, the slum of nations. Think of America as growing up on the toughest block of the roughest ward of an international Hell's Kitchen. Repeat after me, President Obama, "It's a hard street. And it gets harder as it goes along. And I live in the last house." You do. The White House.

Some people are going to expect neighborhood cooperation. They'll tell us, "It takes a village . . ." And it does, if it's a Potemkin village we're after. Yet neighborhood improvement is a worthy goal. We should pursue it. Of course we want a better class of people holding the governmental mortgages on the residences around us. Let's do what we can to encourage them. Lend them some rule-of-law power tools. Help them clean the gutters of democracy when it's raining Islamists and demagogues. Ask them over for a spot of free trade.

We should always keep in mind, however, that the foremost task of foreign policy—be the policy ever so high-minded and altruistic—is to keep the scum of the earth at bay. The job is to ensure that, for whatever time he's got left in his cave, Osama bin Laden spends it cowering. Mahmoud Ahmadinejad must never make it to dawn without coming awake with a start, fearing what's under his bed. And Kim Jong II, we hope, wishes he had Michael Jackson's personal physician to rock him to sleep. We must make Hugo Chávez sweat through his ugly shirts and cause Robert Mugabe to tremble with something more than the palsy of age. When they think of America, Hu Jintao should worriedly consult fortune cookies and Vladimir Putin should be driven to drink.

12

Foreign Policy, Part Two

It Keeps Getting More Foreign

Foreign policy is the most frustrating subject for a political theorist. There is no theory. It's strictly practice. No implicit social contract exists. The explicit contract is the very prefix of negation, UN. And it's all about asshole foreigners.

Freedom becomes subject to outlandish interpretations. Power leaves persuasion in its other suit and packs a gun. And responsibility is something to go pound sand about at the International Court in the Hague. When foreign policy also has to deal with widespread ideologies of terror, no arranged marriage is possible because the fuckers have put aside everything but killing.

Perhaps the best piece of foreign policy advice was given in a speech by then vice president Theodore Roosevelt in 1901 at, of all places, the Minnesota State Fair: "Speak softly and carry a big stick." Teddy was a clamorous mouth-off whose shillelagh school of politics was a disaster to the nation from his charge up San Juan Hill to his Bull Moose destruction of the Taft presidency. Thus there may be something to be learned about foreign policy by listening to people who talk through their hats.

This, like government policy toward the automobile companies, brings me back to Rudyard Kipling. He isn't often a first-rate poet, and, with brilliant exceptions, his prose can be annoying too. But there's something in Kipling that, a hundred years later, speaks to us Americans. Maybe it's because Kipling, like an American, was middle class, a bit of a social misfit, unduly fascinated by gadgetry, had foggy notions about geopolitics, and found himself the citizen of a nation that had become the preeminent power on the globe half by accident. Also, Kipling was scorned by the *bien-pensants* of his era for being an imperialist.

President Obama, I have bad news for you. *You're* an imperialist. I realize that for a young man like yourself, educated in the highest circles of modern academia, what I've said is a grave insult. While I'm at it, let me offend you completely and say that you're carrying "The White Man's Burden." Your foreign policy is an attempt "To veil the threat of terror/And check the show of pride." You've vowed to "Send forth the best ye breed—Go bind your sons to exile/To serve your captives' need." And you've sworn, among other things, to "Fill full the mouth of Famine/And bid the sickness cease." The result of all this will be to—I'll bet you a second term—"Watch Sloth and heathen Folly/Bring all your hope to naught."

Perhaps, Mr. President, you've never read "The White Man's Burden." I doubt they teach Kipling (British, 1865–1936) in the highest circles of academia these days. And I doubt you learned anything about imperialism except that it's an epithet in constant overuse by blackboard bolshevists. To understand this slur that you can't escape you'll have to go back to pre-postmodern academia, before it got high and started going in circles. In the 1940s Hans Kohn, the Sydenham Clark Parsons

Professor of History at Smith College, wrote[54] that "the concept of imperialism carried various connotations in the different
periods of history." According to Kohn, among these connotations is a "liberal" one. We owe it to Alexander the Great. And
it has been recurring intermittently for twenty-four centuries:
"a world state, a cosmopolis, in which all the inhabitants would
live in complete equality, in intermarriage and commercial exchange, on the basis of one common civilization." Sounds like
your Hyde Park neighborhood.

Professor Kohn argued that what nineteenth-century British imperialism connoted was an attempt "to bring the occidental concepts of political liberty and human dignity to oriental
nations." Professor Kohn further argued that "as a result of
its ethical basis, liberal imperialism carried its self-annulment
with it." He was wrong on this last point. Because here are the
British—and us along with them—"somewheres east of Suez"
again, bringing more occidental concepts to oriental nations
whose previous supply seems to be used up.

There is an irony to this. Rudyard Kipling was fond of irony.
And he was considered to be the poet laureate of imperialism when imperialism was still wearing laurels. Mr. President,
maybe you should undo some of the damage from the hours you
wasted as an undergraduate reading Frantz Fanon and Edward
Said and brush up on your Kipling.

Rudyard Kipling was a firm proponent of Kohn's liberal imperialism, so much so that Kipling still had his nose out of joint
about 1776. But he was also a shrewd critic of American politics, as he proved in his poem "The American Rebellion," about
our founding fathers.

---

54. In the article "Imperialism," *Encyclopaedia Britannica*, 1946.

> *Not till their foes were driven forth*
> *By England o'er the main—*
> *Not till the Frenchman from the North*
> *Had gone with shattered Spain;*
> *Not till the clean-swept oceans showed*
> *No hostile flag unrolled,*
> *Did they remember that they owed*
> *To Freedom—and were bold!*

Sounds like your attorney general Eric Holder's investigation of CIA interrogations.

Believe me, Mr. President, you're better off getting your foreign policy perspective from Rudyard Kipling than from Eric Holder. And forget Hillary Clinton. (The way the rest of the world has forgotten Hillary Clinton.) There is, however, one problem with Kipling's perspective. For a positive-thinking young man like yourself, Kipling's views are damn grim. Take for example "The Man Who Would Be King." I realize you weren't assigned the short story, but maybe you remember the movie, with Sean Connery and Michael Caine. Or maybe not. You were fourteen when it premiered and were probably home watching "Maude" and taking notes.

Anyway, Daniel Dravot (Connery) and Peachy Carnehan (Caine) are two mustered-out British noncoms on the skids in the raj. They decide to make their way up past Swat and Chitral (you'll recognize those names from your daily briefings) to a remote mountain fastness called Kafiristan.

Daniel and Peachy think that, with the proper application of Western military technology and Western political science, nation building (perhaps you've heard this before) will be a snap. They do a lot of good, Daniel and Peachy do. They bring peace and prosperity to the Kafiris and reinvigorate the local Free-masonry lodge. And they get their heads handed to them. Or, rather, Peachy gets Daniel's head handed to him, whereupon Peachy crawls back to civilization in much the same condition as George W. Bush crawled back to Crawford, Texas.

It's often assumed that Kafiristan was a place that Kipling invented, using "kaffir," the South African derogatory slang for black, to create a country named (to put it in contemporary terms) "N-Wordland." In fact, Kafiristan was a place high in the Hindu Kush mountains, a pagan enclave in otherwise Muslim territories. "Kafir" means "unbeliever" in Arabic. When Kipling wrote his story, in 1888, Kafiristan had been seen by exactly one European since the time of liberal imperialism's inventor Alexander the Great. Major George Robertson was knighted just for looking at it. Other than the knighthood things did not go well for Kafiristan, as things usually don't in such necks of the woods. Alexander the Great himself came back with an awful wife from the region, Roxanne, her white trash name appropriate since hereabouts is supposed to be the cradle of the Aryan race. In 1895 the locals were forcibly converted from paganism, with much slaughter, by the prematurely Islamo-fascist emir of Kabul, Abdur Rahman. Very foreign places like this are full of people who live far outside the cosmopolis and don't have their world citizenship papers in order. One wonders whether the goings-on in the Kafiristans of the earth are any better understood today than they were when Daniel and Peachy were playing NATO.

Kipling did not believe that "one common civilization" was impossible. He argued that ordinary people, be they ever so different, are at least as much our fellow humans as the Irish. "For the Colonel's lady an' Judy O'Grady/Are sisters under their skins!"

Kipling's "The Ballad of East and West" is remembered for the line "never the twain shall meet." But the story the poem tells is the opposite. A British officer's son lights out after the hill tribe thief who stole his father's horse and comes back a blood brother to the horse thief's son, sort of like Sergeant James Crowley and Skip Gates after your beer summit.

> But there is neither East nor West, Border,
>   nor Breed, nor Birth
> When two strong men stand face to face,
>   though they come from the ends of the earth!

In the 1901 novel *Kim* the hero is obviously of mixed race (thinly disguised as a Euro orphan for the sake of Edwardian miscegenation sensitivities). Kim's mentors are Mahbub Ali, a Muslim Indian of high rank in the British Secret Service, and—what could be more world state modern?—a Tibetan lama. Furthermore, the Freemasonry lodge to which Kipling belonged in Lahore was multicultural and racially diverse, just like Daniel's and Peachy's in Kafiristan (and yours in Hawaii, if you'd stayed there and joined one).

But Kipling also argued that mankind's one common civilization was something the *sahibs* could never grasp. By a sahib, Kipling meant you, Mr. President. In his poem "One Viceroy Resigns," he has Lord Dufferin (viceroy of India 1884–88) tell Lord Lansdowne (viceroy 1888–94; note that neither lasted eight years):

> You'll never plumb the Oriental mind,
> And if you did it isn't worth the toil.
> Think of a sleek French priest in Canada;
> Divide by twenty half-breeds. Multiply

By twice the Sphinx's silence. There's your East,
And you're as wise as ever.

So cloddish is the mental process of officialdom that in Kipling's day it thinks of Quebec as Asiatic. And in our day it thinks of Canada as having an admirable health care system.

As for the profits of imperialism, Kipling was pessimistic in "The White Man's Burden." The poem was published in 1899 as an admonition to President McKinley (and his vice president Teddy Roosevelt) about colonial occupation of the Philippines, spoils of the Spanish-American War. Kipling was yet more pessimistic when he counted profits in pounds, shillings, and pence. With the verses of "Arithmetic on the Frontier" Kipling calculates the time and effort of educating a British officer.

> *A great and glorious thing it is*
> *To learn, for seven years or so,*
> *The Lord Knows what of that and this,*
> *Ere reckoned fit to face the foe*

He estimates how the investment will pay off.

> *A scrimmage in a Border Station—*
> *A canter down some dark defile—*
> *Two thousand pounds of education*
> *Drops to a ten-rupee jezail*

He analyzes the risk/benefit ratio.

> *Strike hard who cares—shoot straight who can—*
> *The odds are on the cheaper man.*

And he presents a chilling imperialist business prospectus.

> *With home-bred hordes the hillsides teem,*
> *The troopships bring us one by one,*
> *At vast expense of time and steam,*
> *To slay Afridis where they run.*

> *The "captives of our bow and spear"*
> *Are cheap, alas! as we are dear.*

Why did Rudyard Kipling support imperialism? He believed in civilization. He believed in liberty, justice, equality before the law, and all the benefits of material progress attendant thereto. Kipling may not have believed in democracy in quite the same way you, Mr. President, and your ACORN community activists believe in it—with one vote, at the very least, for each man, woman, and child. But you, on the other hand, show no signs of believing in any other aspect of civilization. Your health care reform strikes at the very body of liberty from Rogaine head to athlete's foot toe. Your bailout programs exhibit contempt for justice. Your taxation proposals indicate that you consider everyone to be equal before the law until he or she is rich enough to be worth robbing. And your cures for climate change show profound ignorance of the means by which economies grow. It is a poor imperialist, Mr. President, who has no faith in his empire's culture and refinement.

Rudyard Kipling had that faith, and then some. He not only believed in civilization, he believed in civilization as God's will. Those of us who possess liberty, justice, and equality before the law have a sacred duty to extend the hand of civilization even when we get our fingers bitten off. And should we, against all

odds, succeed and see civilization win out across the world, that's
not a glorious triumph for us but a humble fulfillment of obligation. Kipling felt this humility should always be kept in mind, and
on the occasion of Victoria's Diamond Jubilee, at the very high
water mark of the British empire, he said so to the Queen's face:

> *If, drunk with sight of power, we loose*
>   *Wild tongues that have not Thee in awe—*
> *Such boastings as the Gentiles use,*
>   *Or lesser breeds without the Law—*
> *Lord God of Hosts, be with us yet,*
> *Lest we forget—lest we forget!*

Rudyard Kipling was a righteous man. He wasn't always in
the right, by any means, but he was righteous. And we know that
you, too, Mr. President, are righteous—self-righteous. Whether
your righteousness reaches beyond the end of your nose will
be determined by how you treat "Your new-caught, sullen peo-
ples,/Half-devil and half-child." If you treat them with the same
presumptuous arrogance you use on the populace of your own
country, then, Mr. President, you'll have plenty of time in early
retirement to read more Kipling and meditate on the fate of our
particular civilization.

> *Far-called, our navies melt away;*
>   *On dune and headland sinks the fire:*
> *Lo, all our pomp of yesterday*
>   *Is one with Nineveh and Tyre!*
> *Judge of the Nations, spare us yet,*
> *Lest we forget—lest we forget!*

PART III

Putting Our Big,
Fat Political Ass
on a Diet

A democracy cannot exist as a permanent form of government. It can only exist until a majority of voters discover that they can vote themselves largesse out of the public treasury.
        —attributed to Alexander Tytler, Lord Woodhouselee,
                                        Scottish jurist ca. 1800

1

Why I'm Right

Some people arrive at their political convictions through experience, some through study, some through thought. My political convictions are a result of all three, or, rather, the lack of them.

I was brought up in Republican circumstances, firmly grounded in convention. I was swept out to Marxist sea by a flood of sex. I was trying to impress cute beatnik girls. Then, one day, I found myself beached on the shore of jobs and responsibilities and I was a Republican again. No cognition, cogitation, or will seems to have been involved in my ideological spin drift. As both a radical and a reactionary I was formed by history and institutions. All those beatnik girls had a history. Many of them ended up in institutions.

My maternal great-grandfather owned a farm in downstate Illinois. He was a county sheriff, a stalwart of the GOP, a friend of President McKinley's, and a breeder of harness racing horses. His dying words summarize my family's attitude toward the great sociopolitical issues that would shake the twentieth century: "How did Shorty do at the track today?"

His daughter, my grandmother, was ten when she began accompanying her father to the Republican Party's political conventions in Chicago. She never got over the shock of that blowhard easterner Teddy Roosevelt splitting the party and allowing such a man as Woodrow Wilson—from a Confederate state!—to become chief executive. As far as my grandmother was concerned, Taft was the last real Republican. In a moment of childish innocence I once asked her what the difference was between Republicans and Democrats. She said, "Democrats rent."

My father's family was, if anything, more Republican. My paternal grandfather was a widower, left with a business to run and six small children on his hands. He remarried more in haste than wisdom. The stepmother was insane. She left Uncle Joe out on the back steps until his diapers froze. Grandpa divorced her. But, then as now, there was a political aspect to getting an annulment. (The Kennedys seem to have a vending machine that dispenses them.) According to family story, Grandpa O'Rourke and the local bishop clashed and Grandpa went out and, in one day, joined the Methodist church, the Freemasons, and the Republican Party. He had a heart attack just before the 1960 elections. At the funeral his sister, my great-aunt Helen, said, "It's a good thing your grandfather died when he did. It would have killed him to see John Kennedy president."

Thus my life would have gone along perfectly well, politically speaking, if it hadn't been for girls. I found them interesting. They found me less so. On my first weekend at college I was walking down an alley with a bar on either side. Each bar had a patio full of students. The girls on one patio were very attractive, their sweaters well filled, their pleated skirts worn daringly above the knee, their blond hair styled in what was called a "sorority flip." They sipped demurely from beer mugs decorated with Greek letters.

But I wasn't athletic or handsome or a Sigma Chi legacy. And I had a feeling that, even if I were, getting such girls into bed would involve attendance at mixers and dances, romantic chat-ups, fumblings under coats in the shrubbery while house mothers tsked out windows, bestowals of one's fraternity pin or even an engagement ring, and lots of talk about "our future."

The girls on the other patio were fetching as well, in their black leotards and peasant blouses, denim skirts, and sandals. Their long, dark hair was ironed straight. They strummed guitars, smoked unfiltered cigarettes, and drank beer straight from the bottle. I thought, "I'll bet those girls do it."

They did. I went home at Christmas break with my hair grown long, wearing a blue jean jacket with a big red fist emblazoned on the back. My grandmother said, "Pat, I'm worried about you. Are you becoming a Democrat?"

"Grandma!" I said. "Lyndon Johnson and Richard Nixon are both fascist pigs! Of course I'm not a Democrat! I'm a communist!"

"At least you're not a Democrat," said Grandma.

Having donned the clown costume I found it easy to honk the dogma nose, squirt the progressive seltzer, and pile into tiny cars (VW bugs). Soon I really was a communist unless I really was an anarchist or an anarcho-syndicalist or a Trotskyite or a Maoist. I never read any work of political ideology unless by accident, because it was assigned in class. And then I studied it as perfunctorily as any Sigma Chi in the lecture hall. Nothing ensures an obliviousness to theory like the need to get a passing grade on a quiz about it.

I have ex-leftist friends who recall long, intense, fractious political arguments during their university years. But I was at Miami of Ohio, not Berkeley or Columbia. My college friends and I may have begun such discussions, but then the rolling papers were brought out and the debate became over where to get Mallomars.

However, inchoate ideas are often more deeply held than any others. Emerson, for instance, believed intensely in his conception of metaphysics even though, on inspection, he didn't have one. And it's often forgotten what instinctive communal levelers and utopians kids are. After all, they're raised in the only successful Marxist economic organization on earth, the family. Outside the home, children spend their formative years under authoritarian, antimaterialistic regimes at school, catechism, summer camp, and Little League. They're taught sharing and caring and "fairness" and a kind of toadying social equality (". . . it's how you play the game"). They're given employment consisting of involuntary volunteer work to fulfill their Boy Scout, or church, or school, community service requirements. Maybe they get a job doing some mindless sorting at dad's friend's FedEx store. They are "part of the solution" and/or they experience proletarian alienation. Then they're sent off to college to learn about freedom and responsibility—freedom to get naked and stoned and responsibility to turn down their stereo after one a.m. It's a wonder that anybody under twenty-five is even a Mikhail Gorbachev.

In my day there was also the war in Vietnam. Proponents of the present war in Afghanistan (myself included) should consider the effect that certain armed conflicts can have on the ideologically impressionable (whether at Berkeley or a Kabul madrassa). Wars need clear arguments of justification, clear strategies of execution, clear objectives. P.S., they need to be won. And the impressionable can't be left wondering just who the winners were. World War I was a dilly in all these respects with ideological consequences less trivial than those of the 1960s.

The Vietnam War's military draft lent extra solipsism to the self-cherishing melodrama of being an adolescent. The government was intent on interrupting my fun to send me to some distant place with a noxious climate to shoot people I didn't know, and, what was worse, they'd shoot back. I had a stepfather at home whom I was perfectly willing to shoot while he snored on the couch. But the government was insensitive to my needs.

I stayed a left-winger for more than a decade. This despite at least three Road to Damascus moments when I should have been converted to better views. During graduate school in Baltimore I worked on an "underground" newspaper. We shrilly denounced war, injustice, and this and that. One evening our office was invaded by a group of young people more radical than ourselves who felt that our denunciations weren't shrill enough. They called themselves, and I am not kidding, the Balto-Cong. They accused us of being capitalist roaders and said they were liberating the oppressor's private property in the name of the people. We explained that they were welcome to it, the private property consisting of about ten thousand dollars of debt, three typewriters, and an old row house from which we were about to be evicted. (Radicals are rather worse than Democrats; they not only rent but are in arrears on their rent payments.) We were held at knuckle-point and made to undergo a consciousness-raising session that might have gone on who knows how long if a couple of "the people" hadn't stopped by. These were two teenage black kids from the neighborhood. They asked, "What the hell's going on here?" and scared the Balto-Cong away. The neighborhood kids were honors English students who hoped the underground newspaper would provide a venue for their poetry. And I'm glad to say that, thereafter, it did.

A fellow ex-staffer at the newspaper (now also a Republican) tells me that I spent the rest of that night slamming my fist into a beanbag chair and saying, "Spiro Agnew was right!" But I got over it. I had realized there were bad people on the left, but I hadn't realized I was one of them.

Then my student deferment ran out and I was drafted. Standing in my underwear at the draft physical I noticed that I and all the other hirsute children of privilege were clutching thick folders of doctors' letters about asthma, neurosis, back problems, and being allergic to camouflage. The poor kids, with their normal haircuts and the discount store Y-front briefs that came up over their navels, were empty-handed and about to be marched off to war. This told me something about what my radicalism was doing to benefit the masses. But I forget what, because the army doctor told me something more interesting. He told me to get out of there. The army had no use for drug-fuddled hippies.

I remained determined that wealth should be shared with everyone, especially me. But the silent majority tacitly refused to agree and I had to get a job. The pay was $150 a week. I was to be paid every two weeks. I was eagerly looking forward to my check for $300 dollars (as was my landlord). But when payday came I found that, after withholdings for federal, state, and city income tax, Social Security, health insurance payments, and pension plan contributions, I netted about $160. I'd been struggling for years to achieve socialism in America only to discover that we had it already.

Usually when I'm asked what made me a Republican I tell that story. But it isn't true. I mean the story is true, but it didn't really change my mind. I went on for years considering myself to be at least a nominal leftist.

I was too busy to be involved in left-wing causes anymore. I had that job. And, truthfully, all causes are boring. They are a way of making yourself part of something bigger and more exciting, which guarantees that small, tedious selves are what a cause will attract. Plus I was finding my work to be about as big and exciting a thing as my own small, tedious self could handle.

And I had begun to notice something else about left-wing causes. Radicals claim to seek what no one claims to want. The collective has been tried in every conceivable form from the primitively tribal to the powerfully Soviet, and "the people" who are thus collectivized immediately choose any available alternative, whether it's getting drunk on Indian Reservations or getting shot climbing the Berlin Wall.

I'd enjoyed all the left-wing rioting. Better yet had been the aftermath back at the crash pad. "We've got to get this tear gas off us. We'd better double up in the shower, Sunshine, to conserve earth's natural resources." But the rioting, along with the Vietnam War, was petering out. Still, I was a man of the left. That was the sort of person I admired. Rick, in *Casablanca,* was a man of the left, and, uh, Rick in *Casablanca* . . . Anyway, nobody gets misty-eyed singing "I dreamt I saw Bill Taft last night/ As fat as he could be . . ."

In the end it was silliness, not sense, that turned me back into a Republican. One day in the middle 1970s I was walking along a street and my reflection was caught at an odd angle in a store window so that I saw myself without realizing who I was looking at. I was wearing dirty jeans and a work shirt with mystic chick embroidery on it and a thrift shop peacoat, and my hair was all over the place. I thought, "That guy's looking pretty silly for somebody his age."

Silliness made me a Republican, and boredom helped too. My aging hippie friends were boring. They continued to be convinced that everything was going to be shared soon, so they hadn't gotten jobs. They hadn't gotten married either, although wives were the one thing that did seem to be getting shared. Occasionally they had a kid. They didn't let the diapers freeze. There weren't any. These children, though provided with remarkable freedom from discipline and conformity, didn't seem to give much thanks for it, or ever say thanks, or please, or even "How are you?" My friends were living the lives of unfettered bohemian artists. Except the lack of fetters seemed to tie them to dumps on the Lower East Side. (Rented, not owned.) And where was the art?

These people not only had a great capacity to be boring, they had a great capacity to be bored. Imagine a talent for ennui so well developed that you could be bored by God. It's futile for a political radical to believe in God because politics has all of God's power to shape life and then some. God recused himself in the matter of free will. Radicals do not. Then there's the egotism of the idealist. If the problems of the world can be intellectually solved by me, what's the intellectual need for Him? Furthermore, the wicked world is so full of wrongs, which radicals are trying to right, thereby making radicals better than that no-good God who created the wicked world. Or would have if He existed. God's like, you know, a square.

My own lack of religious faith persisted even after I'd renewed my faith in other things such as buying instead of renting. If I could summon enough faith to vote for the average Republican, which, by the early 1980s, I was doing, I certainly should have been able to summon enough faith for the Apostles' creed. But the selfish leftist habit of doubt stayed with me. In 1984 I was in Beirut writing an article about the Lebanese civil war. My friend Charlie Glass, ABC's Middle East correspondent, dragged me out into the Beqaa Valley to interview a terrifying man named Hussein Mussawi, head of a violent fundamentalist Shi'ite militia called Islamic Amal. Mussawi looked at me and asked—in English, which he had theretofore shown no signs of speaking—"Do you believe in God?" I remember wondering if I was fibbing when very quickly I said yes.

Then one day it seemed futile *not* to believe in God. Maybe existence was pointless, though it did have its points for me— writing books, fixing up the house I'd bought in New Hampshire. I'd started hunting again. I'd learned to ski. Maybe I was just too small a part of creation to understand what the larger point was. But if I was so small that my comprehension was meaningless, what did that make my incomprehension? Also, although I could imagine that existence was pointless, I couldn't imagine that it was accidental. Existence seemed too intricately organized. Having led an accidental existence for years I knew that such an existence was intricate, maybe, but organized? Never. (Note how often leftists need to admonish themselves with the slogan "Organize!") If the random forces of quantum physics were all that was in play then these forces had dropped butter and eggs and mushrooms and cheese and a Zippo on the kitchen floor and gotten an omelet. Whether I like omelets was neither here nor there.

★ ★ ★

On the other hand, it was just such an incredulity about things somehow organizing themselves that kept me from embracing all the implications of the free market. "Laissez-faire" was a personal attitude long before I gave it larger significance. Then I remembered a lesson of my leftist days: "The personal is the political." And I began leaving other people alone not only in my life but in my mind.

By the early 1990s my political philosophy was completely elaborated. I didn't have one. I simply thought—and I continue to think—that it is the duty of every politically informed and engaged person to do everything he or she can to prevent politics.

But I was not yet a conservative. I was a Republican and a libertarian. The mutual exclusivity of those two political positions was, I thought, one more proof of the self-negating nature of politics, which should be allowed to take its course until politics is regarded as such a nugatory enterprise that people have to be chased through the streets and tackled and forced to serve as senators, representatives, presidents, and Supreme Court justices. Or maybe, I thought, there should be a game of governance tag where someone has to stay a congressman or senator until he's able to catch someone else and make him "it." If this means legislative halls filled with the helpless and crippled so much the better.

I still think it's a good idea. But that is not conservatism. I became a conservative at 11:59 p.m. on December 4, 1997, the way many people become conservatives. My wife gave birth. Suddenly I was an opponent of change.

Every change was filled with danger. If the temperature in the baby's room changed, I worried. If the temperature in the baby changed, I agonized. Changing my shoes became a matter of great anxiety. Better go to work in my slippers—any noise could wake Muffin. I was tortured by the change from a child who sat up to a child who crawled. Was her speed of development too slow? Was her speed headfirst into the table leg too fast? The change from crawling to toddling was terrible. I wanted to stand with William F. Buckley athwart the tide of history shouting, "Don't swallow the refrigerator magnet!"

Things that once were a matter of indifference became ominous threats, such as refrigerator magnets and homosexuality. I used to consider erotic preferences a matter of laissez-faire. Then I realized, if my children think homosexuality is acceptable, it could lead them to think something really troubling, that sex is acceptable. Daddy has been down that alley. It took me years to figure out how to be a Republican again. There will be time enough for my kids to learn the facts of life from the priest during Pre-Cana counseling. As for public education's "tolerance" curriculum, the heck with *Heather Has Two Mommies*. How about *Heather Has Two Nannies*. There's a book that could teach children something worthwhile in the way of values.

I have lost all my First Amendment principles about rap songs lyrics. I am infuriated by them. Because I cannot understand a word that hip-hop musicians say. For all I know what's spewing out of their mouths is, "We need a single-payer national health care system," or, "Home mortgage interest tax deductions subsidize suburban sprawl, increase the burden on transportation infrastructure, and lead to greater production of greenhouse gases."

I am appalled by violence on TV, specifically the absence of it on PBS. "Which perfectly harmless thing is Caillou terrified of today?," I always ask my six-year-old, Buster. "Why isn't Caillou ever terrified of something sensible like a pit bull? Why don't his parents just give him a whack when he whines?"

And what if a purple Tyrannosaurus rex shows up in my backyard? The kids will run outside expecting to play games and sing songs and they'll be eaten. What kind of lessons is PBS teaching our children?

Being a parent means suddenly agreeing with Pat Buchanan about everything except immigration. For Pete's sake, Pat, nannies are hard enough to find. Not that I want to do away with Barney, Snoop Dogg, or love (whether it can't speak its name or can't shut up). I am a true conservative. I hate *all* change.

The most recent presidential campaign was won on a campaign of "hope and change." I was appalled about the change part. We had just, finally, gotten Buster out of diapers. Change is not a good word at our house. Or anywhere else. Change a tire. "You'd better change your ways." Change of life. Any change in a wart or mole.

And hope's no better. You remember your Greek mythology. The box that hope comes in is Pandora's box. After Pandora opens that box and death and disease and all the ills that plague mankind have been loosed upon the world, nothing is left in the box but hope. Is it a good thing when you've got nothing left but hope? How about when you've got nothing left but hope for a government bailout?

Conservatives want things to remain static, to stay just the way they are, not because these things are good but because these things are *there*. When I have to deal with things I know where they live. Conservatives are opposed to change not because change is bad but because change is new. It's as modern and confusing as the metric system or the BlackBerry. I don't know how to count the change. And I can't find the OFF button for the hope.

One last thing about change—it's different. No one without children knows how fraught the word "different" is. When used about your child it's never good news. When used by your child it isn't either. If a kid says, "You're different," he means you're crazy. If he says, "I don't want to be different," he means he's going to skip school and shoplift. And when "the spaghetti tastes different" he's about to throw up.

Radicals wish to make a difference. To the born-of-parenting conservative this sounds as sensible as wishing for head lice.

The conservative parent feels the same way about those small, itchy things called ideas. Radicalism is the pursuit of ideas. (A pursuit that, for me, was made all the more tantalizing by the fact that I never came close to grasping one.) Any conservative can tell you that ideas have consequences. Who wants consequences? Conservatism is a flight from ideas. As in, "Don't get any ideas," "What's the big idea?," and "Whose idea was that?"

A flight from ideas might sound like Philistinism but think how valuable the above phrases are when used on children. Or politicians. And what's so bad about being a Philistine? Putting religious prejudice aside, the Philistines seem to have been respectable people who did well in business. For all we know the reporting on the David and Goliath battle comes to us from some Old Testament version of NPR. And David, what with the poems, the messy love life, the increased centralization of government, was too liberal for my taste.

Furthermore, ideas are not to be confused with facts. One of the great things about being a conservative is that when a decision has to be made—for example, is hiding your spinach under your dinner plate and then trying to feed it to the dog right or wrong?—facts can be consulted. Is it a cardinal sin? A venial sin? Against the law? Or you can just ask mom. A radical can't do this, no matter how many moms are extant. Radicals have to work everything through de novo. Radicals have ideas about sin, law, and motherhood. And the more airy the ideas, the more the answer has to be pulled out of thin air (and the more spinach the dog gets, which doesn't make the dog happy either).

The great moral principles of conservatism, if not self-evident, have at least been entered into evidence by thousands of years of human experience. And the great political principles of conservatism are simple, summarized by the important and perceptive political philosopher Walter Kowalski, portrayed by Clint Eastwood in the movie *Gran Torino*: "Get off my lawn." Then there are the great intellectual principles of conservatism, which are, mmm . . .

Some years ago I was enjoying the conservative pleasures of a driven pheasant shoot in Ireland. Among my hunting companions was a wonderful old fellow named Preston Mann, now pursuing game in paradise. Preston was one of the world's great dog trainers, the proprietor of a splendid hunting club in Michigan, and a crack shotgunner. I'm none of these, in particular the last. I kept missing the pheasants with my first barrel. I generally picked them up with a second shot, but bird after bird escaped my initial blast. Preston was shooting from the next butt and, midst the flap and crackle of pheasants winging toward us, he turned to me and shouted, "P.J. you're thinking about it. It ain't a thinking man's game."

Where the Right Went Wrong

Speaking of thoughtless, on November 2, 2008, conservatives negligently misplaced a twenty-eight-year period of opportunity to prove the merits of conservative politics in America. A completely unknown and somewhat unctuous political tyro from nowhere was elected president in preference to an experienced, respected, and well-liked Republican war hero. (And not for the first time, even since 1980, per the somewhat unknown and completely unctuous Bill Clinton). The '08 presidential defeat was accompanied by an utter destruction of the remaining conservative power in Congress.

The victory of liberalism is temporary, as all democratic political victories are. Our political system cannot be owned, it can only be (my grandmother says thank you, Democrats) rented. But there is something instructive in the disappearance of the late conservative ascendency—carried away by a bear market, a Bear Stearns, and the bear that headed into the woods to shit on conservative political philosophy.

An entire generation has been born, grown up, and had families of its own since Ronald Reagan was elected. And where is

the world we promised these children of the Conservative Age?
Where is this land of freedom, empowerment, and responsibility, plus knowledge, opportunity, accomplishment, honor, truth,
trust, and one tedious hour each week spent in itchy clothes at
church, synagogue, or mosque? It lies in ruins at our feet, as well
it might, since we our conservative selves kicked the shining city
upon a hill into dust and rubble. The progeny of the Reagan
revolution will live instead in the universe that revolves around
the Hyde Park neighborhood of Chicago.

Mind you, they won't live *in* Hyde Park. Those leafy pre-
cincts will be reserved for the micromanagers and macro ap-
paratchiks of liberalism—for the secretary of the Department
of Sweetness, the secretary of the Department of Light, and the
secretary of the Department of Making Everything Fair. The
formerly independent citizens of our previously self-governed
nation will live, as I said, *around* Hyde Park. They will make
what homes they can in the physical, ethical, and intellectual
slums of the South Side of Chicago.

The South Side of Chicago is what everyplace in America
will be once a liberal administration and a liberal Congress
have tackled climate change, sustainability, green alternatives
to coal and oil, home mortgage foreclosures, consumer protection, business oversight, financial regulation, health care reform,
urban sprawl, and tax increases on all the people who are rich
because they're making more than the (soon to be raised!) minimum wage. And don't be too sure that liberals won't have plenty
of time to do all this, because conservatism, if it's ever really
reborn, will not come again in the lifetime of anyone old enough
to be rounded up by ACORN and shipped to the polling booths.

I do not blame the left. After the events of the twentieth
century—national socialism, international socialism, interspecies

socialism from Greenpeace—anyone who is still on the left is obviously psychotic and not responsible for his or her actions. No, we on the right did it. The financial crisis that hoisted us on our own petard was only the latest (if the last) of the petard hoistings that ensued from the hindparts of our movement. We had nearly three decades to educate the electorate and we responded by creating a big city public school system of a learning environment.

Liberalism had been running wild in the nation since the Great Depression, and at the end of the Carter administration we had it cornered in one of its dreadful housing projects or smelly public parks or some such place, and we held the Taser gun in our hand, pointed at the beast's swollen gut, and didn't pull the trigger.

Liberalism wasn't zapped and carried away in an ambulance and confined somewhere until it expired from natural causes such as natural law or natural rights.

We didn't kill liberalism because that would have meant killing power. And we wanted the power for ourselves. Nor did we offer therapy to the public for its crippling liberalism. Successful treatment would have meant a public cured of its dependence on government. Which was now us.

We never tried, in words or deeds, to convey to the electorate the universal and organic nature of freedom. Thus we ensured our loss before we even began our winning streak. Barry Goldwater was an admirable and principled man. He took an admirably principled stand on states' rights. But he was wrong. Separate *isn't* equal. Ask a kid whose parents are divorced.

Since then modern conservatism has been plagued by the wrong friends and the wrong foes. The Southern Strategy was bequeathed to the Republican Party by Richard Nixon, not only a wrong friend of conservatism but no friend at all. The Southern Strategy wasn't needed. Southern whites were—begging the pardon of the Scopes trial jury—on an evolutionary course toward becoming Republican. There's a joke in Arkansas about a candidate hustling votes in the country. The candidate asks a farmer how many children he has.

"I've got six sons," the farmer says.

"Are they all good little Democrats?" the candidate asks.

"Well," the farmer says, "five of 'em are. But my oldest boy, he got to readin' . . ."

There was no need to piss off the entire black population of America to get Dixie's electoral votes. And despising cracker trash who have laundry hampers full of bedsheets with eyeholes in them does not make a man a liberal.

Blacks used to poll for the party of Lincoln. They did so right up until Mrs. Roosevelt made some sympathetic noises in 1932. And her husband didn't even deliver on Eleanor's promises.

It's not hard to move a voting block. And it should be especially easy to move voters to the right. All sensible adults are conservative in most aspects of their private lives. If this weren't so, imagine driving on the freeway. The majority of the drivers are drunk, stoned, making out, or playing video games on their cell phones while the rest are trying to calculate the size of their carbon footprint on the back of Whole Foods receipts while negotiating lane changes. It's LA.

People with children are, as has been noted, even more conservative. Nobody, except maybe one pothead in LA, is a liberal with the kids. Everybody wants his or her children to respect freedom, exercise responsibility, be honest, get educated, have opportunities, and own a bunch of guns. (The last is optional and includes, but is not limited to, me, my friends, and Todd Palin.)

Reagan managed to reach out to blue collar whites. But there his reach stopped, leaving many people on the conservative side but not knowing it. There are enough yarmulkes among the neocons to show that Jews are not immune to conservatism. Few practicing Catholics vote Democratic anymore except in South Boston where they put something in the communion wafers. When it comes to a full-on, hemp-wearing, kelp-eating, mandala-tatted, fool-coifed, echt liberal, I have never met a Muslim like that or a Chinese and only a few Hispanics. No U.S. immigrants from the Indian subcontinent fill that bill (the odd charlatan yogi excepted) nor do immigrants from Africa, eastern Europe, or East Asia.

We conservatives have all this going for us. Yet we not only let conservatism be portrayed as a fringe ideology, we used that portrayal as a marketing strategy. Of course the trailer park God brothers vote Republican. If you're handling rattlesnakes and keeping dinosaurs as pets, would you vote for the party that gets money from PETA?

In how many ways did conservatives fail conservatism? Even the guy at the General Accounting Office who's in charge of calculating the national debt can't count that high. Take just one example of our unconserved tendency to poke our noses into other people's business: abortion. Democracy, be it howsoever conservative, is a manifestation of the will of the people. We may argue with the people as a man may argue with his wife, but in the end we submit to the fact of being married. Get a pro-life friend drunk to the truth-telling point and ask him what happens if his fourteen-year-old daughter gets knocked up. What if it's rape? Some people do have the courage of their convictions. I don't know if I'm one of them. I might kill the baby. I *will* kill the boy.

The real message of the conservative pro-life position is, as the prefix indicates, that we're in favor of living. We consider people—with a few obvious exceptions—to be assets. Liberals consider people to be nuisances. People are always needing more government resources to feed, house, clothe them, pick up the trash after their rallies on the National Mall, and make sure their self-esteem is high enough to join community organizers lobbying for more government resources.

If the citizenry insists that abortions remain legal—and, in a passive and conflicted way, the citizenry seems to be doing so—then give the issue a rest. Meanwhile we can, with the public's blessing, circumscribe the timing and method of taking a human life, make sure parental consent is obtained when underage girls are involved, and tar and feather teenage boys and run them out of town on a rail. (Or we could try a compromise between abortion rights and Second Amendment rights. Good news for liberals, abortion stays legal. Good news for conservatives, the fetus has a gun. Or, if we really want to end the abortion debate in a way that makes everyone happy, we can make abortion retroactive. Wait until the kid's eighteen and if he's still a prick . . .)

The law cannot be made identical with morality. Scan the list of the Ten Commandments and see how many could be enforced even by Rudy Giuliani. "Honor thy father and thy mother." My daughter Muffin would get the chair.

Our impeachment of President Clinton was another example of placing the wrong political emphasis on personal matters. We impeached Clinton for lying to the government. To our surprise the electorate gave us cold comfort. Lying to the government: it's called April 15. And we accused Clinton of lying about sex, which all men spend their lives doing, starting at fifteen bragging about things we haven't done, then on to fibbing about things we are doing, and winding up with prevarications about things we no longer can do.

When the Monica Lewinsky news broke my wife set me straight. "Here," she said, "is the most powerful man in the world. He's not absolutely ugly. And everyone hates his wife. What's the matter with Sharon Stone?" Instead, he was hitting on the emotionally disturbed intern barely out of adolescence. But our hornrims were so fogged with detestation of Clinton that we couldn't see how truly detestable he was. If we had stayed our hand in the House of Representatives and treated the brute with shunning or interventions to make him seek help, we might have chased him out of the White House. (Although this probably would have required an American news media from a parallel universe.)

Such things as letting the abortion debate be turned against us and using the gravity of the impeachment process on something that required the fly swat of pest control were strategic mistakes. Would that blame could be put on our strategies instead of ourselves.

"Politics shouldn't be the first resort" is a fundamental principle of conservatism. Therefore another fundamental principle of conservatism is "Issues that are mostly social shouldn't be turned into issues that are completely political."

★ ★ ★

We have lived up to no principle of conservatism. After our
twenty-eight years government was bigger than ever. We fat-
tened the stalled ox and hatred therewith rather than dining on
herbs where love (and the voter) is. Instead of flattening the Department of Education with a wrecking ball we let it stand as a
pulpit for Bill Bennett. When—to switch analogies again—such
a white elephant is not discarded someone will eventually try to
ride in the howdah on its back. One of our supposed own did.
No Child Left Behind? What if they deserve to be left behind?
What if they deserve a smack on the behind? A nationwide program to test whether kids are what? Stupid? You've got kids.
Kids are stupid.

We railed at welfare and counted it a great victory when Bill
Clinton confused a few poor people by making the rules more
complicated. But the "French bread lines" for the banks, the
"terrapin soup kitchens" for the investment firms continued to
dispense charity without stint.

The sludge and dreck of political muck funds flowing to
prosperous businesses and individuals grew deeper and more
slippery and stank worse than ever with conservatives minding
the waste treatment works of legislation.

Agriculture is a business that has been up to its bib over-
alls in politics since the first Thanksgiving dinner kickback to
the Indians for subsidizing Pilgrim maize production with fish
head fertilizer grants. But never, since the *Mayflower* knocked
the rock in Plymouth, has anything as noisome as the Farm,
Nutrition, and Bio-Energy Act of 2008 been spread upon the
land. Just the name says it. There *are* no farms left. Not like
the one Grandma grew up on. "Farm" today means a hundred

thousand chickens in a space the size of a Manhattan studio apartment. If we cared anything about "nutrition" we would, to judge by the mountainous, jiggling flab of Americans, stop growing all food immediately. And "bio-energy" is a fraud of John Edwards's marital fidelity proportions. Taxpayer money is composted to produce a fuel made of alcohol that is more expensive than oil, more polluting than oil, and tastes almost as bad as oil with vermouth and an olive. But this bill was passed with bipartisan majorities in both houses of Congress and was happily signed into law by President George W. Bush. Now it will cost us at least $285 billion. That's about five times the gross domestic product of prewar Iraq. For what we are spending on the Farm, Nutrition and Bio-Energy Act of 2008 we could have avoided the war in Iraq and simply bought Saddam Hussein's damn country.

Yes we got a few tax breaks during the regimes of Reagan and George W. Bush. But if you make over $209,000, your tax rate is still about one third of your income. Now 209 long is nice money. But it's not exactly Wild Willy Gates income territory. Here you are working hard, doing well, making America strong and prosperous, and the government is taking a third of your pay. Is the government doing a third of your job? Is the government doing a third of your dishes? Your laundry? Your vacuuming? When you go to Hooters is the government tending bar, making sure that one out of three margaritas is on the house? If your spouse is feeling romantic and you're tired does the government come over to your house and take care of foreplay? (Actually, during the Clinton administration . . .)

Anyway, a low tax rate is not—never mind the rhetoric of every conservative politician—a fundamental principle of conservatism. The principle is fiscal responsibility.

Conservative politicians should never say to voters, "We can lower your taxes." Conservative politicians should say to voters, "You can raise our spending. You, the electorate can, if you choose, have an infinite number of elaborate and expensive government programs. But we, the government, will have to pay for those programs. We have three ways to pay.

"We can inflate the currency, destroying your ability to plan for the future, wrecking the nation's culture of thrift and common sense, and giving free reign to scallywags to borrow money for worthless scams and pay it back ten cents on the dollar.

"We can raise taxes. If the taxes are levied across the board, money will be taken from everyone's pocket, the economy will stagnate, and the poorest and least advantaged will be harmed the most. If the taxes are levied only on the wealthy, money will be taken from wealthy people's pockets hampering their capacity to make loans and investments, the economy will stagnate, and the poorest and the least advantaged will be harmed the most.

"And we can borrow, building up a massive national debt. This will cause all of the above things to happen plus it will fund Red Chinese nuclear submarines that will be popping up in San Francisco Bay to get some decent Szechuan takeout."

Yes, this would make for longer and less pithy stump speeches than "I'll cut taxes!" But we'd be showing ourselves to be men and women of principle. It might cost us, short term. We might get knocked down for not whoring after bioenergy votes in the Iowa caucuses. But at least we wouldn't land on our scruples. And we could get up again with dignity intact, dust ourselves off, and take another punch at the liberal bully boys who want to snatch the citizenry's freedom and tuck that freedom, like a trophy feather, into the hatbands of their greasy political bowlers.

But *are* we men and women of principle? And I don't mean in the matter of tricky and private concerns like gay marriage. Civil marriage is an issue of contract law. Constitutional amendment against gay marriage? I don't get it. How about a constitutional amendment against *first* marriages? Now we're talking. No, I speak, once again, of the fundamental principles of conservatism.

Where was the *meum* and the *tuum* in our shakedown of Washington lobbyists? It took a Democratic majority in the House of Representatives forty years—from 1954 to 1994—to get that corrupt and arrogant. And we managed it in just twelve. (Who says Republicans don't have much on the ball?)

Our attitude toward immigration has been repulsive. Are we not pro-life? Are not immigrants alive? Unfortunately, no, a lot of them aren't after attempting to cross our borders. Conservative policies on immigration are as stupid as conservative attitudes toward immigrants are gross. Fence the border and give a huge boost to the Mexican ladder industry. Put the National Guard on the Rio Grande and know that U.S. troops are standing between you and yard care. George W. Bush, at his most beneficent, said that if illegal immigrants wanted citizenship they would have to do three things: pay taxes, learn English, and work in a meaningful job. *Bush* didn't meet two out of three of those qualifications.

To go from slime to the sublime, there are the lofty issues about which we conservatives never bothered to form enough principles to break. What is the conservative foreign policy?

We may think of this as a post–9/11 problem but it's been with us all along. What was Reagan thinking, landing marines in Lebanon to prop up the government of a country that didn't have one? In 1984 I visited the site where 241 marines and sailors had been murdered by a suicide bomber the year before. It was a beachfront bivouac overlooked on three sides by hills full of hostile Shi'ite militiamen. You'd urge your daughter to date Rosie O'Donnell before you'd put troops ashore in a place like that.

Since the early 1980s I've been present at the conception (to use the polite word) of many of our foreign policy initiatives. Iran-Contra was about as smart as using the U.S. Post Office to deliver democracy to Iran. And I notice Danny Ortega is back in power.

I had a look into the eyes of the future rulers of Afghanistan at a 1989 *sura* in Peshawar while the Soviets were withdrawing from Kabul. I would have rather had a beer with Leonid Brezhnev, dead as he was. At least there would have been beer.

Fall of the Berlin Wall? Being there was fun. Nations that flaked off the Soviet Union in the Caucasus and Central Asia? Being there was not so fun.

The aftermath of the 1991 Gulf War still makes me sick. Fine to save the fat, greedy Kuwaitis and the arrogant, grasping House of Saud, but to hell with the Shi'ites and Kurds of Iraq until they get some oil.

Then, half a generation later, when we returned with our armies, we expected to be greeted as liberators. And damn it, we were. I was in Baghdad in April 2003. People were glad to see us until they noticed that we'd forgotten to bring along anyone to feed or doctor the survivors of shock and awe or to get their water or electricity going again. After that they got cranky and began stuffing dynamite in their pants pockets before consulting with the occupying forces.

Is there a moral dimension to conservative foreign policy? Or is the point just to help the world's rich people make and keep their money? (And a fine job of *that* we've done lately.)

If we do have morals, where were they while Bosnians were being slaughtered? Where were we when Clinton was dithering over the massacres in Kosovo and decided, at last, to send Kosovo's Serbs a message: Mess with the United States and we'll wait six months then bomb the country next to you. About Rwanda I can't bear to think let alone wisecrack.

Then, to carry conservatism on its final trip to the recycling bin, came this financial crisis. For almost three decades we conservatives had been trying to teach average Americans to act like "stakeholders" in their economy. They learned. They cried and whined for government bailouts just like the billionaire stakeholders in Citigroup. Aid was forthcoming. Then average Americans learned the wisdom of Ronald Reagan's statement: "The ten most dangerous words in the English language are, 'I'm from the federal government and I'm here to help.'" Ask a Katrina survivor.

The left had no idea what was happening in the financial crisis. And I honor their confusion. Joe Jerk down the road from me, with the cars up on blocks in his front yard, fell behind in his mortgage payments and the economy of Iceland collapsed. I'm missing a few pieces of this puzzle myself.

Under political pressure that never seemed to be noticed by conservatives, a lot of lousy mortgages, which couldn't be repaid, were handed out to Joe Jerk and his drinking buddies and all the ex-wives and single mothers with whom Joe and his pals have littered the nation.

Wall Street looked at the worthless paper and thought, "How can we make a buck off this?" The answer was to wrap it in a bow. Take a wide variety of lousy mortgages—some from the East, some from the West, some from the cities, some from the suburbs, some from shacks, some from mansions—bundle them together, and put pressure on the bond rating agencies to do fancy risk management math. The result was a "collateralized debt obligation" with a triple-A rating. Good as cash. Until it wasn't.

Wall Street pulled the "room full of horseshit" trick. Brokerages said, "We're going to sell you a room full of horseshit. And with that much horseshit, you just *know* there's a pony in there somewhere."

Anyway, it's no use blaming Wall Street. Blaming Wall Street for being greedy is like blaming prostitutes for getting paid. The people on Wall Street never claimed, as even prostitutes might, to be public servants. Investment bankers took no oath of office. They're in it for the money. We *pay* them to be in it for the money. We don't want our retirement accounts to get a 3 percent return. (Although that looks pretty good at the moment.)

We, the conservatives, who understand the free market, had the responsibility to, as it were, foreclose upon this mess. The market is a measurement, but that measuring does not benefit a nation or its citizens unless the assessments of height, width, volume, and weight are conducted with transparency and under the rule of law. We've had the rule of law largely in our hands since 1980. Where was the transparency?

This is one more fundamental principle of conservatism. It is a political principle, it is an economic principle, it is a principle of manufacturing, finance, and trade. It is a principle that should be kept in mind when you explain to your wife and the people of South Carolina that you disappeared for a week in order to hike the Appalachian Trail. Beyond a certain point complexity *is* fraud.

Think of airline fares. Think of cable service. Think of Microsoft Windows 7. Think of health care reform. Now think of conservatives in government office. It should have been so simple.

A Digression on Shouting at Each Other

American politics has become increasingly polarized and nasty, so I'm told, and conservatives and liberals are shouting at each other too much. I don't think we're shouting at each other enough. I've felt this way for a while, through a great deal of shouting, during an era of partisan clamor so loud sometimes you'd think that, with American politics, it's all over *but* the shouting. I'm satisfied with the quantity of our screeches. Even the quality of our shrieks isn't too bad. But I'm concerned about the direction in which we yell.

I remember the moment I was struck with this concern. It was in the fall of 2003 midst the run-up to the unmemorable presidential election of the following year. The proximate cause was the even more unmemorable General Wesley Clark, who briefly offered himself as the answer in the debate concerning who would be the Democratic Party's candidate for president.

I was driving across the Midwest, listening to Rush Limbaugh shout on the car radio. I usually agree with Rush Limbaugh, therefore I don't tune in to his show. I tune in to NPR: "World to end. Poor and minorities hardest hit." In my own car, with my own radio on, I prefer that it's me who does the shouting.

Of course, if I had continued to listen to Rush Limbaugh over the next few weeks, while his OxyContin addiction was being revealed, I could have shouted at him about drugs. I don't think drugs are bad. I used to be a hippie. I think drugs are fun. Now I'm a conservative. I think fun is bad. I would agree with Rush Limbaugh all the more if, after he had returned from rehab, he'd shouted—as most Americans should—"I'm sorry I had fun! I promise not to have more!" (Or he could have shared.)

Anyway, I couldn't get NPR on my car radio, so I was listening to Rush Limbaugh shout about Wesley Clark. Was Wesley Clark a Hillary Clinton stalking horse?! Was Wesley Clark a DNC-sponsored Howard Dean spoiler?! "He's *somebody's* sock puppet!" Limbaugh shouted.

My laugh was followed by an uneasy thought. Who was Rush Limbaugh shouting at? Was he shouting at Wesley Clark? I doubted that Clark listened to AM talk radio the way I listened to NPR, to get his blood pressure up. Besides, Howard Dean was already doing that for Clark. Was Rush Limbaugh shouting at uncommitted voters, hoping to scare them into the George W. Bush camp? Shouting "Hillary Clinton!" "Howard Dean!" "John Kerry!" over and over might have done it. But what uncommitted voter cared a spit about Wesley Clark? The person hearing the shout had to know enough about Democratic politics to know who Wesley Clark was and enough about Wesley Clark to know that he was a small pumpkin and a false alarm. Was Rush Limbaugh shouting at Hillary Clinton supporters to hearten them? At Dean supporters to energize them? At Kerry supporters to alert them? These people didn't tend to be ditto heads. No, I realized, Rush Limbaugh was shouting at me.

Me. I am a little to the right of . . . Why is the Attila bench-
mark always used? Fifth-century Hunnish depredations upon
the Roman empire were the work of an overpowerful centralization of authority with little respect for property rights, pursuing
a policy of economic redistribution in an atmosphere of permissive social mores.

I am a little to the right of Rush Limbaugh. I'm so conservative that I could talk Ellen DeGeneres out of supporting
gay marriage. Gays wed, they buy a house, they have children,
they encounter the public school system. Then gays all vote
Republican.

I suppose I should be shouting at my fellow right-wingers
about that, and draconian drug laws, and many other things.
Shouting is a form of argument. And the purpose of argument
is to convince others. Many people deny that shouting is a
form of argument. They say, "Nobody ever convinced anybody
about anything by shouting at them." These people don't have
children.

Shouting can be a very effective form of argument, as will
be attested to by any person (say, a president of the United
States) who's heard a sermon preached by the Reverend Jere-
miah Wright. But, when shouting, you must have people within
earshot who—will they, nil they—are receptive to the shout-out.

After I'd realized, in 2003, who Rush Limbaugh was shouting at, I performed an experiment. I listened to some more talk
radio, watched some conservative television programming, and
read some of the conservative books that were popular at the
time. I listened to Michael Savage and Mark Levin. I watched
Bill O'Reilly's *No Spin Zone* and the Sean Hannity part of *Hannity & Colmes*. They did a lot of shouting. But they didn't seem
to be shouting at the potentially repentant sinner who had

guiltily slipped in at the back of the congregation after emptying his bottle of malt liquor. Nor did they seem to be shouting at the abashed political wire puller in the middle pews, his
conscience bothered by the electoral blood on his hands. No,
Limbaugh, Savage, Levin, O'Reilly, Hannity et al. were shouting
at the pious women in the big hats standing blamelessly in the
choir. That is, they were shouting at—with a change of gender
and headgear—me.

I judged the conservative books by their covers (certainly
a better method than reading their reviews, if any, in the *New
York Times*). Ann Coulter, on the cover of *Treason,* had the look
of a soon to be ex-wife who'd just gotten done shouting. And
Bill O'Reilly was wearing a loud shirt on the cover of *Who's
Looking Out for You?* Also, his title was a rhetorical question I remembered hearing shouted by various frustrated scout masters,
camp counselors, and sports coaches. Then I gave the books a
good reading, the same kind of good reading I gave to my textbook *The Democracy of Our Self-Governing Republic* in eleventh-
grade civics class to keep the teacher, Mr. Mannsburden, from
shouting at me.

Ann Coulter's book was subtitled "Liberal Treachery from
the Cold War to the War on Terrorism." Her theses were that the
love of the ideal results in the hatred of the real and that belief in
changing society, totally, means belief in totalitarianism. At least
I think those were her theses. (Understand that I found myself
operating in eleventh-grade essay test mode: "Manifest Destiny.
Manifested? Destined? Discuss.")

In the first paragraph of her book Coulter wrote, "Liberals
have a preternatural gift for striking a position on the side
of treason. You could be talking about Scrabble and they
would instantly leap to the anti-American position. Everyone

says liberals love America, too. No they don't. Whenever the nation is under attack, from within or without, liberals side with the enemy."

Mind you, I'd shouted this sort of thing myself. But it was two in the morning and I was shouting it at a couple of other drunk right-wingers in the bar. Here was Ann Coulter putting it down in black and white on the printed page in the cold light of day. I'm not saying she was wrong, but was this the kind of shouting likely to call anyone in from left field?

The volume was not turned up quite so high in *Who's Looking Out for You?* But there was something of the halftime harangue at the team in just the adoption of that second-person voice. It began with the title and extended from the introduction ("When you finish this book . . . you *will* know what's going on.") to the last page ("You deserve to have good people on your side."). Again, I'd heard myself shouting this, hoarsely, with my eyes misting up, at 2 a.m. in the bar.

Who's Looking Out for You? could be condensed thus: "Nobody, what's who! The fat cats aren't looking out for you! The bigwigs aren't looking out for you! Nobody's looking out for you except me, and I can't be everywhere! You've got to look out for yourself! How do you do that? You look out for your friends and your family, that's how! And they look out for you! And that's the truth, Bud!"

We've all backed away from this shouting guy while vigorously nodding our heads in agreement. Often the shouting guy we were backing away from was our dad.

And O'Reilly, in his book, did come across as dad-like, somewhat pathetically wanting to be listened to and liked and thought of as a decent fellow. He cast his net widely in search of a nodding, agreeing, backing away audience. He attempted to ingratiate himself with people driving pokey economy cars: "Not imposing gas mileage standards hurts every single American except those making and driving SUVs." He gave a nod to folks with a foggy nostalgia for the liberalism of yore: "The gold standard for public service was the tenure of Robert Kennedy as attorney general." He got up on the hobbyhorse of nativism to voice worries about illegal aliens coming across the border and taking jobs from us. (I was worried about illegal aliens *not* coming across the border and *giving* jobs to us, such as painting the house.) And O'Reilly tried to reach out to youth by prefacing each chapter with lyrics from pop groups that, as far as I knew, were hip in 2003, like Spandau Ballet. But the person O'Reilly was shouting at was still me: "If president Hillary becomes a reality, the United States will be a polarized, thief-ridden nanny state with a mean-spirited headliner living on Pennsylvania Avenue."

Fortunately that didn't happen. George W. Bush was no headliner.

My retired FBI agent father-in-law is fond of the shouters. He's a little to the right of, well, me. After I'd listened to the radio, watched the TV shows, and read the books, I asked him, "What do you get out of these loudmouths? You already agree with everything they say."

"They bring up some good points," said my father-in-law.

"That you're going to use on who?" I said. "Do your retired FBI agent golf buddies feel shocked by the absence of weapons of mass destruction in Iraq and want to give Saddam Hussein a mulligan and let him take his tee shot over?"

Whereupon my father-in-law looked at me with an FBI agent look and I shut up.

In the 1960s, a generation before my Limbaugh ah-ha moment, there wasn't much conservative media. ("Media" was a liberal worry word that had just come into vogue, denoting what ordinary people watched, listened to, and read, as opposed to what liberals thought they should.) Mostly it was just William F. Buckley hosting *Firing Line*.

Buckley didn't shout a lot, except at Gore Vidal and who can blame him. But Buckley's icy sarcasm spoke louder than bellowing. William F. Buckley was like Miss Ditwiley, my eleventh-grade English teacher, as opposed to Mr. Mannsburden, my civics teacher. Mr. Mannsburden did a lot of shouting, sometimes to effect and sometimes not. One quiet word from Miss Ditwiley froze you in your seat.

Therefore I count lonely Bill Buckley as a stentorious (as he would have said) voice. And with little but this *vox clamantis in deserto* to guide it, public opinion went from the 1964 defeat of Barry Goldwater with 38.5 percent of the popular vote to the 1980 victory of Ronald Reagan with 50.7 percent of the popular vote.

After Reagan was elected conservative media grew enormously in popularity and range. The result, as far as I could figure it, was nil. In 1988 the less conservative George H. W. Bush was elected with 53.4 percent of the popular vote. By the time we got to 2000, George W. Bush—arguably more conservative than Reagan himself—had to resort to Florida lawyers and a Supreme Court ruling to gain the presidency. One could have, I thought, accused conservative commentators of shouting "Fire!" in a burned-down theater.

I wondered if the left had the same problem. Did liberal commentators say, at the top of their lungs, things that didn't need saying to people who, it goes without saying, didn't need to hear them said? Were there liberals who felt as if they were dogs hearing a human command: "Eat food dropped on the floor!" "Jump up on house guests!" "Bark like a fool at squirrels!"

NPR seemed more whiney than hectoring, except at fundraising time. There was supposed to be a lot of liberal braying on network television. (Network television still existed in 2003.) I watched ABC, CBS, and NBC and looked for things that debased freedom, ridiculed responsibility, and denigrated man and God but that was all of ABC, CBS, and NBC. How did one tell liberalism from the Levitra ads?

Liberals seemed to do their best shouting in print. Michael Moore had published a book not long before, *Stupid White Men,* titled in a spirit of resonant persuasiveness unmatched since *Against the Murderous, Thieving Hordes of Peasants* by Martin Luther (that original antinomian).

Now Moore had another book out, *Dude, Where's My Country?* Employing the stylistic niceties of the hog call, Moore spent ten chapters stridently convincing the stridently convinced. Moore had, however, included an additional chapter on how to argue with conservatives. As if. Approached by someone like Michael Moore, a conservative would drop a quarter into Michael's Starbucks cup and hurriedly walk away. Even assuming Moore had been able to capture the attention of a conservative, I doubted the argument would have gone well. Under the subtitle "Tell them what you *like* about conservatives," Moore suggested the following: "Tell them how dependable conservatives are. When you need something fixed, you call your redneck brother-in-law, don't you?"

Also on the fairly well selling list at the time was Al Franken's *Lies and the Lying Liars Who Tell Them: A Fair and Balanced Look at the Right.* I didn't need to open it. But, having done so, I found these chapters: "Ann Coulter: Nutcase," "You Know Who I Don't Like? Ann Coulter," and "Bill O'Reilly: Lying Splotchy Bully." I supposed these were the sorts of things that liberals shouted at other liberals at two in the morning after the third spliff in the vegan restaurant.

In fairness, however, maybe liberal shouting has been more effective than the kind of shouting my friends and I do. After all, since 2003, Michael Moore has won an Academy Award and a Palm d'Gore—or some such prize—at Cannes. And Al Franken has become a Democratic senator despite, as his stand-up comedian career proved, not being funny enough for it.

Really, I could judge only for my own side. And, while I listened to the ear-splitting racket of the right, my frustration in concurrence built, mounting from an exasperation of like-mindedness to a fury of accord. As a result it's been seven years since I've listened to a damn thing a conservative has said. Going by the snippets of yelping from Sarah Palin that I've involuntarily audited I haven't missed much.

If we're going to shout, let us give people something to shout about. America likes a whoop and holler. There's a little rebel yell in the most confirmed of Yankees. Let us howl in defiance. Let us cut loose with a battle roar. Let us give full throat to a cri de coeur. "You'll have to kill us first!" "Fuck you!" " Marry me!"

4

The Next Big Stink

For the moment, the killjoys[55] are in charge—the mopes, the fusstails, the glumpots. Their wet blanket has been thrown over the White House and Congress. They're worrying up a storm. (Good thing George W. Bush is no longer in charge of the weather the way he was during Hurricane Katrina.)

To sum up America's political situation, we made a mistake. In 2008 we were experiencing a polar ice cap and financial meltdown causing sea levels to rise and sending cold water flooding into Wall Street where the rapidly acidifying ocean was corroding our 401(k)s and releasing mortgage-backed securities full of hot air into the atmosphere until our every breath was full of CO_2 especially when we exhaled, which should be banned when children are present lest their uninsured health care be harmed by secondhand greenhouse gases that endanger plant and animal species (Republicans were declared extinct on January 20,

---

55. In the previous chapter, talking about how conservative I am, I said, "I think fun is bad." I was lying. This is called hypocrisy. I said the right thing, while doing the wrong thing, such as taking drugs with Rush Limbaugh—if he had invited me. Politically, it's a good rule to side with the hypocrites. In matters of right and wrong at least hypocrites know the difference.

2009) leading to a shortage of green, leafy vegetables vital to the fight against America's growing epidemics of obese hunger and housing foreclosures on the homeless. Hence the return of the killjoys.

You remember the killjoys. They're all over liberal Democratic politics like smug on Barney Frank. They initiated automobile crash standards so rigorous that we can't buy a car that hasn't been dropped from the top of a phone pole with our whole family strapped inside. (Click it or Ticket!) And they wrote the infant car seat regulations that require devices so complex, with such arcane rules for use, that each car seat now comes from the manufacturer with its own engineer and each infant comes from the maternity ward with its own lawyer.

Nor is the kid exempt from legislative backseat driving just because she (the pronoun that all publishers with Second Class mailing permits are federally mandated to use in alternate sentences) has emerged from the car. Children must now wear safety helmets to bike, ski, roller-blade, and play hopscotch and wear an additional helmet—in case they collide with hard porcelain and injure their tailbones—on their butts when they go to the toilet. The only time children are allowed to remove their safety helmets is when they catch a parent smoking cigarettes. (Mr. President, you stand warned.) In that case they can doff their protective headgear to better reveal facial expressions of shock, horror, shame, and disappointment. Children learn these facial expressions in the thousand hours of compulsory anti-tobacco education that America's public schools have made time for by eliminating reading and math.

The only way I can sneak a smoke nowadays is to borrow a buddy's hunting cabin in the Maine backwoods, lock myself in the bathroom, and stand in the shower stall with the curtain

pulled tight and the water running. You'd think this would ex-
tinguish my cigar. However, thanks to low-flow shower heads
required by federal law to conserve a precious resource that I
thought we were about to have too much of due to the melt-
ing of polar ice, I can smoke in the shower with the faucets on
full blast and stay bone dry. (Flushing the butt down the water-
conserving john is another matter.)

Sucking the fun out of life has always been an important compo-
nent of politics. The inventors of modern politics, the Puritans
of Cromwell's parliamentary ilk, are rightly a byword for buzz
kill and gloomocracy. The Puritans banned all theatrical per-
formances because of the dangers of . . . they'd think of something . . . actors playing Mercutio and Tybalt having a sword
fight in *Romeo and Juliet* without wearing safety helmets.

Creating alarms about salt content in restaurant food or
energy sustainability in Yellowstone National Park expands the
purview of government almost as well as war, without all the
patriarchal, exclusionist, sexist heroism and hurtful, insensitive patriotic language. Gas prices frighteningly high? Declare
a moral equivalent of Hiroshima. Arteries clogged? Pass a law
requiring the chicken nugget fry basket to be dunked in boil-
ing mint tea.

Raining on parades requires no skill or effort on the part
of a politician. This is what draws people—and Democrats—
into politics. All a politician needs is the upper-story window of
public attention and the chamber pot of rhetoric. How else to
explain that politicians get elected?

Being a poke-nose, a nanny-pants, and a wowser satisfies the
need of the political class to feel self-important and powerful.

Banning paper *and* plastic and making shoppers carry their groceries home in their mouths like dogs is just the thing to make a little tin humanist in the West Wing feel like the admiral of the Mongolian navy.

Not that pecksniff buttinskiism is a strictly partisan matter. Long-lipped howler Republican drys teamed up with spigot-bigot Democrat William Jennings Bryan to enact Prohibition. The Republican Party is home to bluenoses big enough to expand Mount Rushmore with a bust of Andrew Volstead. Republicans stick their snouts into other people's medicinal marijuana prescriptions and underpants (but not gun cabinets). And, when it comes to scolding foreigners and horning in on the governance of lesser breeds without the law, Republicans are a regular pain in the atlas.

Meanwhile Democrats do have their pleasures—drinking bong water at Emily's List fund-raisers and so forth. But it is the Democrats who've best learned to make political honey out of minding other people's beeswax. Not satisfied with mere bossy irritation of the public, Democrats have created whole branches of government—the Department of Labor, the Department of Health and Welfare, the Department of Education, the Department of Tofu and Sprouts. Democrats have opened barrels of (USDA inspected!) pork sufficient to feed all of their high-binding and wire-pulling friends, relatives, and cronies, with table scraps left over for their public sector labor unions. Democratic wisenheimers have managed to get themselves elected Big Chief Itch-and-Rub of every worry and to be appointed Pharaoh of Fret for every concern. They are the party of Eliot Spitzer. And we the citizenry are Eliot Spitzer's wife.

★　★　★

How are the Democrats going to demean and humiliate us next? What issue will the Democrats fasten upon as a threat to the commonwealth and a hazard to the planet? What busybody ordinance and ass-and-elbows regulation will be put upon the books for our own good?

It would be valuable to know the answer. It's important to find out what kind of private enjoyment or human felicity the Democrats are going to pass a law against. We could lobby to defeat it. (Although our best lobbyists are in jail.) We could battle it on principle. (Although our principles, if we ever had any, are on the wane. Witness the paltry vote against the confirmation of Timothy "I forgot taxes were the law" Geithner.) Or we could plan strategies to resist the oppression. (Dig hole behind garage. Buy enormous freezer. Bury the red meat.)

There are several ways to make a prediction about what the Democrats will outlaw. We might calculate the greatest statistical danger to Americans. That would be death. Statistically speaking there is a 1:1 rate of occurrence. But it's hard to build a constituency of dead people, even though they do vote in Cook County. Rahm Emanuel is, we are almost certain, one of the living dead. But whether this gives the White House a pro- or anti-death tilt remains to be seen.

Another way to foretell proscription is to look at the most common or frequently occurring danger to Americans. What causes the most crime, violence, unemployment, divorce, disease, and mental illness? But that brings us back to Andrew Volstead, who was a Republican. Democrats will have to be satisfied with operating on the margins of this issue, providing additional enforcement efforts to curtail Managing a Hedge Fund

While Impaired, etc. Also Democratic Party loyalist trial lawyers can be given legal opportunities, allowing more restaurant and bar patrons to sue for being "overserved." Some friends of mine and I are bringing a class-action suit against P. J. Clarke's in New York where we met our first wives.

In fact, we'd be wrong to use any of the above methods to foresee what our government will attempt to constrain or forbid. A better way to approach the problem is to ask, "What would annoy the most people most often?" That is the true test of government intervention in life. The Secular Grail of the kill-joy is a program or policy that combines the intrusion of the census, the depredations of income tax, the duress of school busing to achieve racial balance, the expense of Social Security, the nuisance of Medicare paperwork, the inconvenience of automotive smog testing, the pettiness of a congressional investigation, and the fine print on the label of flame-resistant children's pajamas.

My guess is that the next great government crusade will be against soap. The president will appoint a Blue Ribbon commission, which will determine that soap releases polluting grime into the ecosystem, leads to aquifer depletion, and contains fatty acids that laboratory studies have shown to be acidic and not fat-free. Soap encourages behaviors that lead to teenage pregnancy as well as adult sexuality with multiple partners, driving America's divorce rate higher, causing more children to live under the poverty line in single-parent households. Soap is a factor in many cases of child abuse, according to small boys in bathtubs. Soap bubbles may contain methane, especially if rising to the surface of bathwater containing small boys. Soap marketing sends the wrong message about the ivory trade and also about Irish spring, which is being altered by climate change. Soap degrades the flame-resistant properties of children's pajamas. And soap makes whales foam when they spout.

Socialism—you can smell it coming.

5

The Fix Is In

We can't change people. We may not even be able to change things. But we can change the way people think about things. Oscar Wilde, in his essay "The Critic as Artist" (1891), wrote, "As long as war is regarded as wicked, it will always have its fascination. When it is looked upon as vulgar, it will cease to be popular." The same can be said about politics.

Wilde's hope for the attitude that people would eventually have toward war seems to have somewhat come true. Once us vulgarians had been convinced that H-bombs would wipe out the entire *vulgus,* we members of that general public were less enthusiastic about war. It hasn't completely lost its fascination, as makers of video games and my six-year-old, Buster, can tell you. But we haven't had any really, really big wars for sixty-five years. Knock wood.

And we haven't had any really, really big politicians since Reagan and Thatcher. Maybe popular taste is changing. Maybe the loud, clashing stripes that politicians wear—reds and blues and pinks and greens with wide streaks of yellow—are beginning to look passé. Maybe the political garb, with its ugly plaid of conflicting interests, its lurid paisley patterns of corruption, and its baggy double-knit of lies, is going out of fashion. And a size XXXL government doesn't fit us anymore. We hope.

We can send politicians to the thrift shop and politics to
Weight Watchers. But we have to be realistic about the new look
that will emerge from this electoral closet cleaning.

I'm sick of politics. We're all sick of politics. We live in a democracy, rule by the people. Fifty percent of people are below average intelligence. This explains everything about politics.

Not that we'd want to live in a country ruled only by the
best and the brightest. That has been tried repeatedly, beginning with Dion, the fourth century BC "liberator of Syracuse,"
who attempted to establish Plato's Republic (and Plato) in Sicily. The outcome was murder and military despotism. Subsequent experiments have produced—*pace* Lenin—worse results.
Even under the ideal systems and circumstances we have in the
United States, being ruled by the best and the brightest would
be like being married to Nancy Pelosi.

Therefore we keep democracy, despite our knowledge that
democracy can go wrong the way it has in Russia, the Gaza Strip,
and Venezuela, not to mention the U.S. House of Representatives.

Politics can't save us. Politics is the idea that society's ills can be
cured politically. This is a cookbook where the recipe for everything is to fry it. The fruit cocktail is fried. The salad is fried. So
is the ice cream and cake. Your bottle of cabernet sauvignon is
rolled in bread crumbs and dunked in the deep-fat fryer. Hence
our big, fat political ass.

Consider how we use the word politics. Are "office politics"
ever a good thing? When someone "plays politics" to get a pro-

motion, does he or she deserve it? When we call a coworker "a real politician," is that a compliment?

Political science, if there were anything even remotely scientific about it, would be searching for a cure.

Still, we're stuck with our politics. The alternative is arbitrary law. We choose to be equal before the law instead. If we're equal before the law, we're equally entitled—to heck with your IQ being higher than mine—to try to shape the law. Are we equal to the task? Of course not. The democratic political process is like the process of our children going through adolescence. There's not much we can do to improve it and there's nothing we can do to stop it. We cannot, however, just declare ourselves to be apolitical any more than we can declare ourselves to be "aparental." Here are the car keys, son. Dad's stash is in the nightstand drawer. Why don't you take my ATM card while you're at it? See you when you're thirty.

"Kill Fuck Marry" is a way to look at politics, but it's also the way politics looks at us. Politics is forever deciding that we shall be murdered, seduced, and entangled in legalities. The only answer to politics is to reduce its power to do these things. Political power can be used to do good and so on and so forth, but there is no excuse for allowing that political power to be concentrated, not even in the most harmless-seeming form—in the form of your beloved infant, innocent as a newborn babe, "trailing clouds of glory/Do we come from God" and all that. Give him unlimited power while he's having a tantrum and he'll destroy the nursery. And the world. No creature could be more blameless and biddable than my Brittany spaniel bird dog, Millie, nor

is she a political incumbent or a registered member of any political party. But endow Millie with infinite might and main? It if
flies, it dies. She would bring down an Airbus A380 and come
back at a trot to drop it at my feet.

Lord Acton's dictum on power is well illustrated in John
Keegan's *A History of Warfare*.[56] Genghis Khan, that political
mastermind, again provides us with an example—as he did with
the American automobile industry. Genghis is supposed to have
asked his warriors what was the most pleasant thing in life. On
being told it was falconry he replied, "You are mistaken. Man's
greatest good fortune is to chase and defeat his enemy, seize his
total possessions, leave his wives weeping and wailing, ride his
horse, and use the bodies of his daughters as bedclothes." The
first Tuesday in November, circa 1200 AD.

Reform movements can't save us. The fallacy of all government
reform was explained by Milton Friedman, "It assumes, somehow, that government is a way that you put unselfish and un-
greedy men in charge of selfish and greedy men."[57]

Members of the first broad-based American reform movement, the Jacksonian Democrats, were right that America wasn't
as democratic as it might be. But under the leadership of their
bloody-minded, Indian-murdering, slave-trading, pigheaded sour
grape of a president, their wanton leveling led to the destruction
of the prototype of the Federal Reserve, the financial destitution
of the country, and the elevation—paradoxically for the

---

56. New York, 1993. Keegan is in turn citing Paul Ratchnevsky, *Genghis Khan*, Oxford, 1991.

57. Radio interview, WIPX in New York, December 7, 1975.

democratic-minded—of the chief executive to the office of mob boss.

The Radical Republicans of the Reconstruction period were wholly right in their attempt to provide freed slaves with enfranchisement and equality before the law. But they let their self-righteousness provoke them into impeaching President Andrew Johnson for opposing them in a fully legal manner. Cambridge historian Hugh Brogan makes the following point.

> Had Johnson been ejected, it would have been for nakedly political reasons, and the whole basis of the Constitutional system would have been overthrown: the principles of co-existent, mutually independent powers; of checks and balances; of laws, not men.[58]

The agrarian-based populist movement of the late nineteenth century, which would come to be led by William Jennings Bryan, was right that high tariffs increased the price of manufactured goods and benefited monopolies and that artificially high interest rates burdened mortgaged farmers. But the populists were so pleased with themselves for pointing out wrongs that it never entered their heads that they were all wrong about righting them. The populists favored debasing the currency, creating inflation, shortening the work day (a hard thing for farmers to do, absent nuclear winter), government confiscation of "excess" land owned by corporations and all land owned by aliens, nationalization of railroads and telegraph and telephone systems, and restrictions on immigration.

---

58. *The Penguin History of the United States*, London, 1990.

The progressives of the late nineteenth and early twentieth centuries, who are with us yet, were intent on finding "scientific" methods of fixing every problem you can think of and some you can't. The attitude of the progressives toward the poor was, says Brogan, "betrayed by the word they used to describe the philanthropic centres they established in the slums, 'settlements': to them the cities were wildernesses, the inhabitants alien savages and the new settlers were bringers both of superior techniques and superior ideas."[59] And, incidentally, bringers of the urban concentration camps we call low-income housing.

One of Theodore Roosevelt's favorite books on politics, *The Promise of American Life*,[60] by Herbert Croly (first editor of the *New Republic,* among his other sins), averred that Thomas Jefferson's vision of America would be achieved by the up-to-date means of centralization and federal cooperation between business and government.

The progressives were important in national politics, especially during the presidencies of Theodore Roosevelt, Woodrow Wilson, and Herbert Hoover, when they prepared the way for the New Deal and liberalism as we know it. But progressives were also important in local government, particularly as big-city mayors such as Hazen Pingree in Detroit (1890–97) and Tom Johnson in Cleveland (1901–9). New York's Fiorello La Guardia (1934–45) fit the mold, and Chicago's Richard J. Daley (1955–76) liked to pretend that he did.

A core thought of progressivism was expressed by Samuel M. "Golden Rule" Jones, mayor of Toledo, Ohio, from 1897 to 1904. Jones was a millionaire turned political reformer who'd

---

59. *Penguin History of the United States.*

60. Published in 1909 and very boring.

made his money building oil well pumps at the Acme Sucker Rod Company (really its name). Jones said in his book *The New Right*,[61] "The Competitive system is the cause that constantly horrifies us and shocks our finer sensibilities with its outrages upon the weak and incapable brothers of society."

Who is to mediate this unfair competition and meliorate its unjust outcome? Woodrow Wilson had the answer in his book *Constitutional Government in the United States*.[62] Even before Wilson was the president, Wilson knew it was the president.

> Let him once win the admiration and the confidence of the country, and no other single force can withstand him, no combination of forces will easily overpower him. His position takes the imagination of the country. He is the representative of no constituency, but of the whole people.

And thus political reformers elevate the chief executive to something more than mob boss and closer to führer.

Individual politicians can't save us either. Democracy means electing people. Politicians are the people who get elected. I've spent some time with politicians. I like politicians. I'm friends with politicians from both sides of the aisle. Politicians are fine until they stick their noses into things they don't understand, such as most things. Then politicians turn into rachet-jawed purveyors of monkey doodle and baked wind. They are piddlers

---

61. Published by the Eastern Book Concern in New York in 1899 and even more boring.

62. Published in 1908 and more boring yet, if that's possible.

upon merit, beggars at the doors of accomplishment, thieves of livelihood, envy-coddling tax lice applauding themselves for giving away other people's money. They are lapdogs of demagoguery returning to the vomit of collectivism. They are pig herders tending that sow who eats her young, the welfare state. They are muck-dwelling bottom feeders growing fat on the worries and disappointments of the electorate. They are the ditch carp in the great river of democracy. And that's what one of their friends says.

What's bad for us is good for politicians. They line up to lick our wounds. They love it when we're hurt. Politicians resemble my fellow journalists and me in this respect. A few years ago I was in a shopping center and a local TV news crew ran in the door looking excited. I asked what was up. They told me there was a large propane tank across the way and it had sprung a leak. I said, "Well, I guess this wouldn't be the moment to step outside and have a smoke."

And the cameraman said, "*Please,* go ahead. We worship different gods than you do." Politicians worship different gods than you do.

Politicians lie to us. But it's not as if they have a choice. Think what the truth would sound like on the campaign stump, even a little bit of truth. Think what would happen to the candidate who said, "No, I can't fix public education. The problem isn't inadequate funding or overcrowding or teachers' unions or lack of computer equipment in the classroom. The problem is your damn kids."

And yet one of our abiding problems with politics is that we insist on blaming our political problems on those politicians. We think lousy politicians are what's wrong. We got rid of George W. Bush, and we have peace in Afghanistan, love in Iraq, and the unemployment rate is at 2 percent.

★ ★ ★

Politicians, by their nature, seek opportunities for political power. They search for problems that only politics can solve. Throw them out the door of social justice and they climb down the chimney of climate change. And see how "global warming" has been deftly transformed by politicians into "climate change," in case the globe fails to warm up. Politicians will be needed in every kind of weather.

If it happens that no problem exists, this acts as a stimulus to political problem solving. The puzzle of public policy making, when public policy isn't needed, spurs a politician to find a more complicated puzzle solution.

America is much richer than it was in 1970. Our per capita gross domestic product (in constant 2000 dollars) was $18,391 forty years ago and $38,262 in 2008. Therefore, obviously, we require fewer federal subsidy programs. Requirements, as you may have noticed, play no part in politics. In 1970 there were 1,019 federal subsidy programs; in 2008 there were 1,804.[63]

The Brady Campaign to Prevent Gun Violence has been lobbying, politically, for tougher firearms purchase and registration laws for a quarter of a century. The Brady Campaign rates states according to how tough those laws are. In 2008 Utah, Alaska, and North Dakota were involved in a tie for forty-third place. California was rated number 1. New Jersey was rated number 2. The number of murders committed with firearms in California in 2008: 1,487. The number in New Jersey: 236. Utah:

---

63. Cato Institute Tax and Budget Bulletin no. 56, April 2009, figures cited from *Catalog of Federal Domestic Assistance*, Government Printing Office, Washington, D.C., 2008.

19. Alaska: 13. North Dakota: 0.[64] Considering the number of reasons there are for shooting people, I'd say Alaska, Utah, and North Dakota need more and cheaper guns.

Lest you think that the political business of brewing trouble, no matter the lack of ingredients, happens only in America's oddball political system, I give you a December 20, 2009, *New York Times* story about our sister democracy France. A Frenchwoman posted an online comment about France's secretary of state Nadine Morano, calling Morano a liar. The punworthy Morano subpoenaed the Frenchwoman's Internet protocol address, discovered her identity, and sued her for "public insult toward a member of the ministry," an offense punishable by a fine of up to $18,000.

In response to the Frenchwoman's protest at her treatment, Jean-François Copé, the parliamentary head of France's ruling party, the bowelishly named Union for a Popular Movement, said, "The Internet is a danger for democracy." How to cope with the likes of Copé the people of California seem to know, the Brady Campaign be damned.

The best politicians can be victims of their own moral over-reaching, even if they avoid the pitfalls of reform ideology and the other pits that politicians fall into. But individual politicians are, after all, individuals like the rest of us and should be judged individually. It would be wrong—very tempting, but wrong—to think of them all as simply bastards. (Although the occasion

---

64. U.S. Department of Justice, FBI Criminal Justice Information Services Division, Crime in the United States 2008, table 20, Murder by State, Types of Weapons.

for temptation is so great that, if we had to make a general rule about politicians, we should probably give in to the tempting.)

In fact, Hazen Pingree, Tom Johnson, Samuel M. "Golden Rule" Jones, and Fiorello La Guardia were good mayors for their time and place. Ronald Reagan was a good enough president. Margaret Thatcher was a good enough prime minister. Mikhail Gorbachev himself, by Russian standards, had something to recommend him in declining to kill people in wholesale lots.

In the 2,500-year history of democracy since ancient Athens, a few politicians have arisen who more or less could be trusted with great powers, up to a point, briefly, in times of dire crisis, sort of. There were Washington, Lincoln, Churchill, and maybe somebody else but I can't think who.

We mustn't expect, or desire, a single politician who will extract us from our political difficulties. The semilegendary Cincinnatus of fifth century BC Rome is often held up as a model politician. An impoverished farmer, though aristocratically born, Cincinnatus was twice given a dictatorship when Rome was in danger and twice, when the danger had passed, promptly resigned the dictatorship and returned to his plowing. Our politicians should return to their plowing—usually of campaign aids. But Cincinnatus is also recalled as an opponent of the plebeians (us) and as a man who resisted enactment of a code of law applicable equally to plebeians and patricians.

We shouldn't go looking for heroes in our politics, although finding an occasional decent man and sticking him into office is no bad thing. To give an example, a politician who I think is okay is John Sununu, my former New Hampshire senator and the son of previously quoted Governor Sununu. I think Sununu is okay not because I agree with him on political issues, though I mostly do, but because of his political philosophy. For starters, he has one. "But it's not," he told me in an interview in 2008, "something I have written down on an index card."

He then proceeded to give me a political philosophy that could be written down on an index card: "We are a free people who consented to be governed. Not vice versa."

If we want to fill the other side of the index card, Senator Sununu said: "In most parts of the world there never has been an appreciation for that perspective. Governments have evolved to provide greater freedom, to reduce the power of monarchies, to reduce absolute power."

When they have evolved at all. I asked Senator Sununu if other politicians in Washington have political philosophies. "There are many," he said, "that would make the argument that they have a core set of values. But these values don't reflect a philosophy. Rather, they reflect a personal goal. 'I believe government should be fair and just,' 'I believe government should represent both the strong and the weak in America.' They're describing characteristics of what they'd like the government to be. They aren't describing principles of organizing a government."

Did Senator Sununu have to compromise his principles to get elected? He said, "Voters are intelligent enough to understand that they can't agree with you about everything. What people want is someone who's thoughtful, direct, and able to explain. Reagan *reveled* in explaining. Was he 'too simplistic'? He was as deep and thoughtful as any of his contemporaries."

Senator Sununu didn't claim to be proud of being a politician. "I'm intrigued," he said, "by the notion that most of our country's founders were suspicious of anyone who wanted to hold public office, e.g., Aaron Burr. The founders retained that

suspicion even after they themselves held public office. They regarded it as an obligation, not an aspiration."

Sununu had held office for a dozen years, first as a congressman, then as a senator. I asked, "Are you suspicious of yourself?"

"When the New Hampshire House seat came open," he
said, "I looked at the other people who had announced. I came
to the conclusion that if I didn't run, New Hampshire would be
represented by another trial lawyer."

The Democrat who defeated John Sununu in 2008, former
New Hampshire governor Jeanne Shaheen, is not a trial lawyer
—her husband is. Shaheen is a product of the only institution
capable of making our lives more miserable than the law courts.
She was a schoolteacher.

After the interview Senator Sununu took me on a tour of the
Capitol building. There are actually two domes atop the Capitol,
one inside the other, and you can climb up in between them, 288
feet, to a little terrace at the feet of the heroic scale figure of Freedom. The view seems to command the world. And sometimes
American politics seems to try to do the same. This is not the best
place to contemplate consent of the governed. But, on the way
up, we'd stopped at the balcony that surrounds the base of the
inner dome. I looked at Constantino Brumidi's fresco *Apotheosis
of Washington,* painted in 1865. I wondered if the tourists in the
Capitol rotunda, 180 feet below, could see how fabulous the al-
legorical and mythological babes are who surround the Father of
Our Country and hover over the proceedings of our democracy.
Armed Freedom (Brumidi's beautiful wife was the model) triumphs over Tyranny and Kingly Power. Enticing Ceres rides a
mechanical wheat reaper while nubile Young America, wearing

a liberty cap and little else, offers her encouragement. Alluring
Aphrodite rises from the sea holding the Atlantic telegraph cable.
And gorgeous Minerva imparts wisdom to Samuel Morse, Robert Fulton, and a frankly smitten Benjamin Franklin. The curva-
ceous arc at the apex of our national headquarters is covered in
4,664 square feet of rosy bosoms, shapely limbs, firm tummies,
and concupiscent hips. We need to get closer to this.

What has to change in America is our minds. And our politicians
need to sit down and shut up, devote their energies to the kind
of thoughts that Minerva has Ben Franklin thinking. Meanwhile
we should be cavorting with the nymphs of our freedoms and
the equally attractive—in their mature way—personifications of
our responsibilities, and not be asking favors from the Tyranny
and Kingly Power of politics. Governance can be party time, as
it is on the Capitol ceiling, but it's BYOB.

The power of politics is based on a fallacious understanding
of "rights." We have to give up all our ideas of positive rights,
gimme rights. To get rid of our positive rights we have to embrace our duties. The helpless and hapless don't have a right to
our assistance, but we have absolute, inescapable—unalienable,
if you will—duties to assist them.

Why do we have these duties? If your conscience can't tell
you, I sure can't. Even if the requirements of duty could be ra-
tionally explained, the elaborate logical justification for the ne-
cessity of duties would be blown to flinders by the thought of life
in a world that didn't have them.

What, exactly, are the duties that we have? And how much
of them? The political process is one of the ways that we attempt
to figure this out.

We are married to our duties. There's no divorce. And, whether we like it or not, politics will always be involved in the execution of our duties. We can be charitable to the point of self-abuse and politics will still be involved. In a big country, and a bigger world, our political system—our arrangement among persons—is such that those who need our help may be too distant in place or circumstance for us to know them the way we know our bum brother-in-law. Our fellow citizens may have to politically inform us of our duties, the way the abolitionists did in the nineteenth century.

Along with our duties of the loving kind, we have less tender-hearted duties to keep our trash picked up, our fires fought, our miscreants arrested, and our criminal and civil courts operating. Annoying as the government's legal monopoly on deadly force can be, we really don't want to privatize it. We've seen privatization of deadly force: 9/11. We can desocialize some other aspects of government but there are limits. It's hard to imagine the advantage of competing networks of private sewer pipes.

Beside compassionate and quotidian duties, there are other responsibilities we need to accept. The adolescent ass who lives near me doesn't have a "right to education." No such right exists. And, personally, I don't feel much of a duty to educate this jerk who, while playing "mailbox baseball" by leaning out the passenger window of a buddy's car and swinging a Louisville Slugger, knocked my U.S. mail receptacle for a triple. But using my money to provide the drip with as much education as he can contain may allow him to put his talents to better use in the future. I'll grant he has some. I myself, in 1964, leaning out the passenger window of a buddy's car and swinging a Louisville Slugger, failed to remember that Mr. Norbert, next door, had put a cement block in his mailbox.

Educating the young is not a matter of rights or duties but it is a good idea, and it's our responsibility to occasionally have one. Either we embrace responsibilities or they get turned over to the Committee Brain of politics.

As I write it's committee brain season in New Hampshire. Town meetings are held in March, as are the meetings of most school boards. There's nothing else to do this time of year, nevertheless few people in their right minds attend these gatherings. I guiltily confess we ought to.

The results of the town meetings aren't too bad, probably because federal and state governments have usurped so much local authority that there isn't much bad left for town meetings to do. Examining the budgets of the town governments in my area, I see that annual expenditure averages about $900 per resident. That's not an exorbitant amount to keep our roads plowed and patched, our playground tetherball poles free from Americans with Disabilities Act violations, and our local malefactors under the eye of the law. (Typical police log entry, as reported in the region's weekly newspaper: "Monday, Feb. 22—At 4 p.m., police received a report of a juvenile throwing rocks at people. Police spoke to the mother. No further action was required.")

The school boards are another matter. The proposed 2010 operating budget for my local school district is $43,698,819. The district has 3,151 students. That's $13,868 per student. The schools are good schools, as they should be for the price. Yet if we hugged our responsibilities tighter we could gather these students into groups of fifteen (the district's high school has a teacher/student ratio of 1:15), employ a tutor for each group, and pay that tutor $200,000 a year. We could hire Aristotle.

True, the kids wouldn't have band practice, but they'd have Aristotle.

But, if we really want to do something good for America our best option is to get rich. Let's say we become a Wall Street financial whiz, making $10 million a year just churning derivatives. And let's say we try our best to cheat the IRS too. We're still going to end up paying—what with income, capital gains, property, and sales taxes—a couple of million per annum into the public coffers. Let's say we do this for twenty years before we're arrested. That's $200 million worth of road repair, trash pickup, help to the disadvantaged, and lethal CIA drones.

Now let's say we don't become a Wall Street financial whiz and join Earth First! instead and spend the next twenty years chained to a tree protesting something. For $200 million we could have bought the damn forest.

Whether we think politics is a bother or whether we are full of great expectations about all the good things politics tries to do, we have to scale back the scope of politics. Otherwise no good things will be accomplished. We can't treat the American government like mom, expecting her to get us off to kindergarten in the morning, fix our meals, wash the dishes, fold the laundry, keep our house clean and our grandparents happy, do the shopping and the gardening, and still somehow make herself interesting to dad. That's why mom snapped and started drinking and got in that car wreck.

6

All Hands On Deck

Of course there's a lot of pent-up energy and aspirations in politics and politicians. And we do want to keep the political system busy and feeling fulfilled, lest politicians get loose in the neighborhood and do real harm.

I think we should provide politics with an important mission, something that will allow politicians an outlet for their love of bombast and glory seeking, that will get them outdoors and give them some exercise. Maybe the political system will slim down.

My idea is pirates.

For a breath of fresh air there's nothing like the bounding main. The flap of canvas, the thunder of cannons, and the clang of bucklers being swashed will surely appeal to our overimaginative politicos. And getting everyone in our government to fight pirates will also silence peevish critics of the political system like me. All mutinous impulses on a ship of state are quelled by the sighting of a hoisted Jolly Roger.

We need pirates. And we're in luck. There's a whole country full of them ready at hand. Thank gosh for Somalia. In April 2009, when Captain Richard Phillips of the *Maersk Alabama* was rescued from Somali pirates by U.S. Navy SEALs, I hoped, for a moment, that the Obama administration would be completely distracted by pirates and forget the rest of its idiot ideas.

Here was the first unblemished American military victory since 1991. And even in Kuwait we stopped short and stood around pulling our mandate while Saddam Hussein slaughtered all resistance to his regime. The Gulf War had nothing like this neat, clean *pop, pop, pop*—with three wicked freebooters sent to Davy Jones's locker and another captured and hauled into the dock, there to face stern justice for brigandage upon the high seas.

Admittedly our bloodthirsty sea dog prisoner, Abduwali Abdukhadir Muse, was notable mostly for sheepish grin, confused mien, and appearing to be about twelve. Still, I don't think we gave President Obama enough kudos for his pirate-fighting triumph. We should have lit bonfires, set off fireworks, and crowned the president with laurel leaves, just to let him know that fighting pirates is the sort of thing that politicians should be doing.

Fighting pirates is bipartisan. Fighting pirates is a consensus builder. Even the Democratic Party is not so inclusive that there's a pirate voting bloc that must be appeased. And if we have to gather all the hundred-foot yachts once owned by AIG executives and now in possession of the Troubled Assets Recovery Program and send these to the Horn of Africa to lure the Somalis from their pirate lairs, so be it.

What an improvement over the other challenges the political system faces. Pirates don't invest in hedge funds, credit swaps, or toxic mortgage debt. Major pirate financial institutions never collapse and require infusions of government funds, because pirates bury gold doubloons in treasure chests and leave us maps marked with an X so we can dig up the gold and replenish the Federal Reserve without recourse to painful tax increases. Plus, if pirates *do* want a bailout, just toss them a rusty bucket.

Pirates have no need of health care reform. Eye patches, peg legs, and hooks are available over the counter at pharmacies, lumberyards, and hardware stores. Other pirate maladies may be treated by shaving their bellies with a rusty razor. Pirate retirement communities are nearby, within easy walking distance. And the planks are wheelchair accessible.

Foreign policy is a moot point. Pirates are men without a country. Never mind that the country they're without is Somalia. "You call that a country?" is the expert assessment we will receive from those with knowledge of the region between Mogadishu and Djibouti. Thus pirates don't have to be sent off to the Hague to be sentenced to ninety days for genocide (time off for good behavior).

The use of pirates for political purposes has a long and happy history. The young Julius Caesar—inexperienced and previously elected to only minor public office—made his mark in the res publica by killing pirates. They captured him on a voyage to Rhodes. Caesar told the pirates that as soon as he was ransomed he would come back and slay every man jack of them, from captain to cabin boy. It will amaze modern politicians but Caesar kept his campaign promise.

Queen Elizabeth I, deft at courting public opinion, was hell on Spanish pirates, when she wasn't busy financing English pirates such as Sir Francis Drake.

Thomas Jefferson sent Stephen Decatur after the Barbary Coast pirates. It was a PR coup. The marines are still going on about "the shores of Tripoli." It worked out well for Decatur too.

There's a whole town in Illinois named after him (more than can be said for a certain former junior senator from that state).

Our politicians should be warned, however, that the victory over the Barbary Coast pirates was frittered away in negotiations with the bashaw of Tripoli. These were conducted by striped-pants cookie-pusher Tobias Lear, U.S. consul general in Algiers. When Lear realized what a screw-up he was, he committed suicide (a protocol that may be worth reintroducing at the Clinton State Department). Therefore President Obama must not be allowed, as is his wont, to *talk* to the pirates. Pirates get to open their mouths only to taste cold steel.

Pirates could make for a turning point in American political life. Yo ho ho and a bottle of . . . Well, the Somali pirates are Muslims. Yo ho ho and a cheekful of khat. Johnny Depp is even now holed up in the Hollywood Hills—an actor prepares—getting ready to play the role of Abduwali Abdukhadir Muse, lone survivor of the attempt to commandeer the *Maersk Alabama*. And Disney's new "Pirates of the Gulf of Aden" attraction will be quite a thrill for the kiddies. There'll be live AK-47 fire and rocket-propelled grenade explosions. Bales of cash from cowardly shipping companies and timorous European nations will fly in every direction. The ticket takers being hired are plainclothes Israeli security guards armed to the eyeballs. And, at the end of the ride, an imam will jump out of the dark and scare the dickens out of the children with a harangue on Islamic fundamentalism.

This imam is not to be confused with Iman the supermodel, now Mrs. David Bowie, although she too is of Somali extraction. And here is another thing that will serve to distract politicians—Somali pirate lasses. Somalia, whatever its other deficiencies, is

full of incredibly beautiful women. In Somalia a girl like Iman
is the girl that the hot girl brings with her to the khat shop so
that the hot girl looks even hotter by comparison. (Not that I'm
implying our president would be interested in this sort of thing,
unlike the previous Democratic president.)

Somali corsairs will grab the fancy of the political establishment and sidetrack the politically engaged from nosing around
in our private business. Sunday morning public affairs TV show
bookers, talk radio hosts, NPR reporters, and the like will be
jamming satellite phone lines to Eyl, Hafun, Obbia, and other
buccaneer redoubts trying to get Somalia's ocean marauders
to change their names to something that's easier to pronounce
such as Blackbeard, Calico Jack, Long John Silver, or Johnny
Depp.

Everybody loves pirates. Do kids ever put on eye shades,
pull out laptops, and pretend to be policy wonks? Did Robert
Louis Stevenson write *Tax Revenue Island*? In *Captain Blood,*
was Errol Flynn portraying an innocent hero forced to become
a New Deal brain truster and team up with Works Progress Administration cutthroat Basil Rathbone? Does Jimmy Buffett sing
"A Liberal Looks at 50"?

I have an even better idea. Politicians, especially liberal politicians, could *be* pirates. They've already got some piratical ideas
for the IRS. As a matter of fact, there was one pirate, a Captain
Misson, who (according to the eleventh edition of the *Encyclopaedia Britannica*) "was unique in combining active piracy
with socialistic ideals. He reigned for many years over a Utopian republic in Madagascar." A good place for the bunch of
them.

Male liberals would have an excuse for wearing an earring. The liberal president could dump his stupid Portuguese water dog (talk about a name for a bad pirate movie) and get a parrot that sits on his shoulder. Every time Glenn Beck comes on TV the parrot would squawk, "Voices of Hate! Voices of Hate!"

Politicians could work the pirate angle a lot of different ways. It's not like just being a politician where you're pretty much locked into one plotline. You become popular. You become unpopular. You become a lobbyist. Piracy is more flexible. Politicians could fly away to J. M. Barrie's Neverland where good triumphs and evil gets eaten by a crocodile. Barack Obama is Peter Pan. Dick Cheney is Captain Hook. Eric Holder is a ticking reptile.

Or politicians could play it for laughs and steal the script from Gilbert and Sullivan's *Pirates of Penzance*. The operetta ends with a daytime television–like scene—an Opraetta!—where it turns out that the privateers are actually well-educated people from prosperous backgrounds, but they have issues, like Nancy Pelosi. In fact the part of Ruth, "a Piratical Maid of all work," is perfect for Nancy Pelosi.

Nancy Pelosi

> One moment! Let me tell you who they are.
> They are no members of the common throng;
> They are all congressmen who have gone wrong!

(I've rewritten the libretto slightly, with Harry Reid in place of the Pirate King.)

President Obama

> No American can hear this and not make amends,
> Because, with all our faults, we love our congressmen.

I pray you, pardon me, ex–Senator Reid,
Pols will be pols, and hacks do have their needs.
Resume your ranks and legislative duties,
And take my daughters, all of whom are beauties.

The president will want to cut that last line. But it will be a great show. Best of all, we'll get to hear Obama sing:

I am the very model of a Democratic president,
With plenty of ideas vague, expensive, and irrelevant,
What I'm saying may be nonsense but I'm saying it emphatical,
What I'm doing may be lousy but pretend it is pragmatical.

The locusts have no king, yet they go forth

—Proberbs 30:27